Warm-Ups

for the Advanced Cellist

Book One

by Cassia Harvey

CHP200

©2008 by C. Harvey Publications® All Rights Reserved.

www.charveypublications.com - print books & free sheet music blog
www.learnstrings.com - PDF downloadable books & chamber music

Warm-Ups for the Advanced Cellist

Scale Patterns · **1** · Cassia Harvey

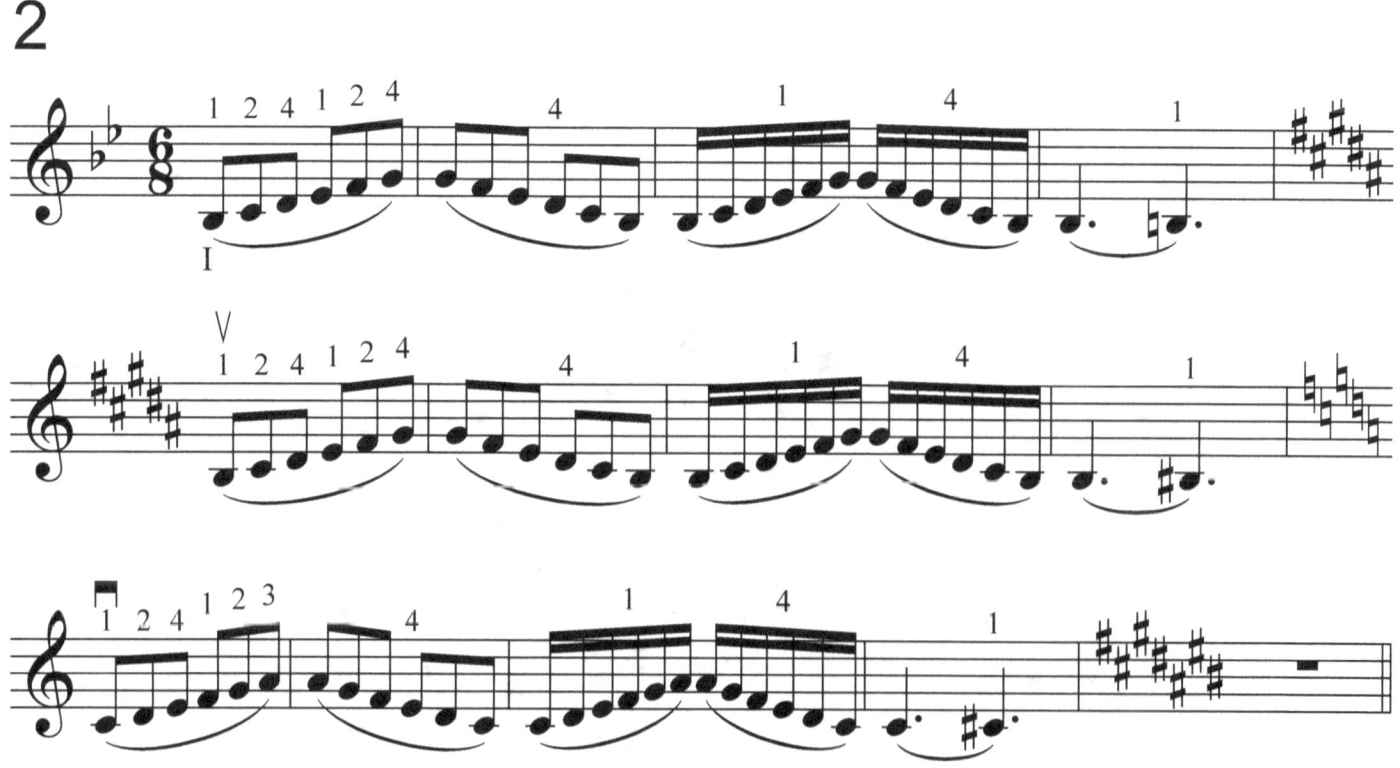

Continue playing the pattern and moving up the fingerboard in half steps, changing the key each time the pattern is played.

2

Continue playing the pattern and moving up the fingerboard in half steps, changing the key each time the pattern is played. When the exercise reaches fifth position, substitute 3rd finger for 4th finger.

©2018 C. Harvey Publications All Rights Reserved.

Warm-Ups for the Advanced Cellist, Book One

3

Continue playing the pattern and moving up the fingerboard in half steps, changing the key each time the pattern is played. When the exercise reaches fifth position, substitute 3rd finger for 4th finger.

4

Continue playing the pattern and moving up the fingerboard in half steps, changing the key each time the pattern is played. When the exercise reaches fifth position, substitute 3rd finger for 4th finger.

©2018 C. Harvey Publications All Rights Reserved.

Warm-Ups for the Advanced Cellist, Book One

5

Continue playing the pattern and moving up the fingerboard in half steps, changing the key each time the pattern is played. When the exercise reaches fifth position, substitute 3rd finger for 4th finger.

6

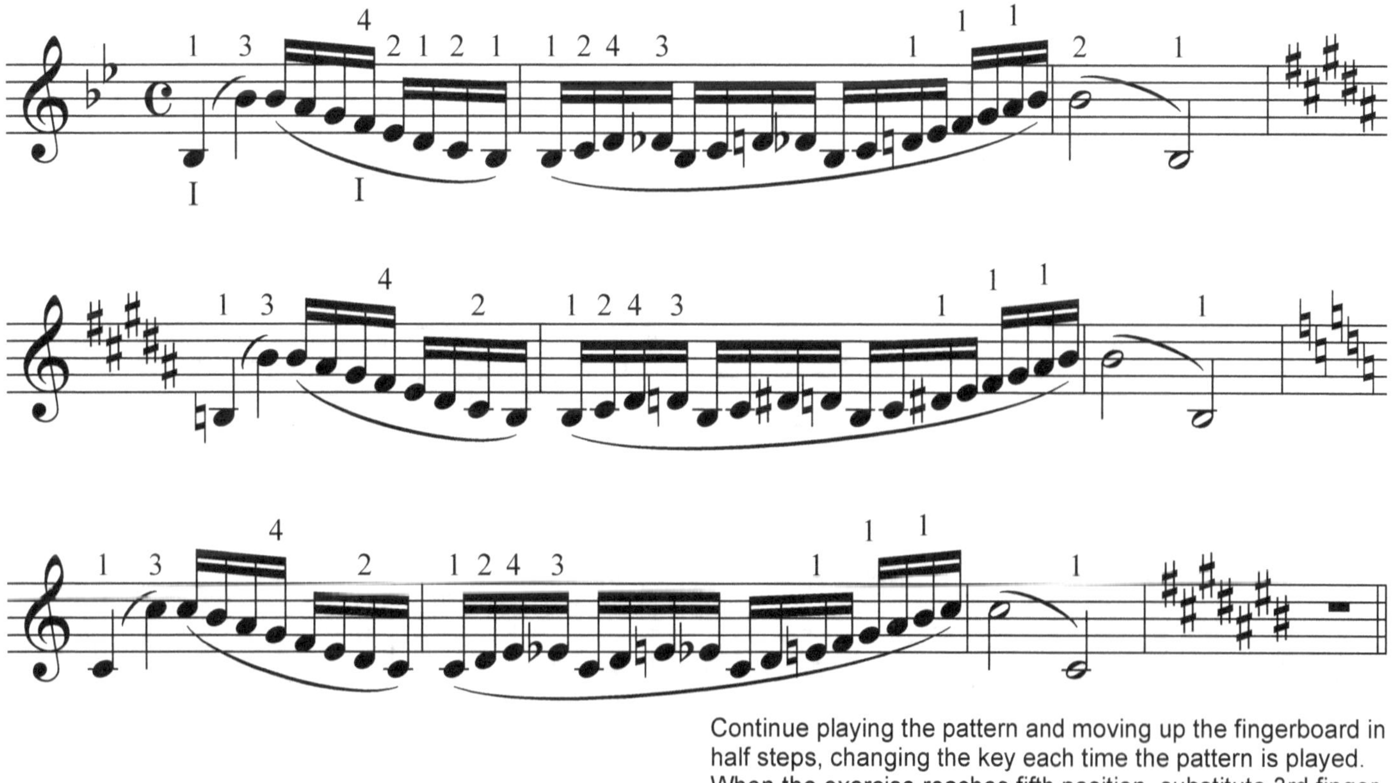

Continue playing the pattern and moving up the fingerboard in half steps, changing the key each time the pattern is played. When the exercise reaches fifth position, substitute 3rd finger for 4th finger.

©2018 C. Harvey Publications All Rights Reserved.

Warm-Ups for the Advanced Cellist, Book One

7

Continue playing the pattern and moving up the fingerboard in half steps, changing the key each time the pattern is played. When the exercise reaches fifth position, substitute 3rd finger for 4th finger.

8

vibrato

Continue playing the pattern and moving up the fingerboard in half steps, changing the key each time the pattern is played. When the exercise reaches fifth position, substitute 3rd finger for 4th finger.

©2018 C. Harvey Publications All Rights Reserved.

Warm-Ups for the Advanced Cellist, Book One

9

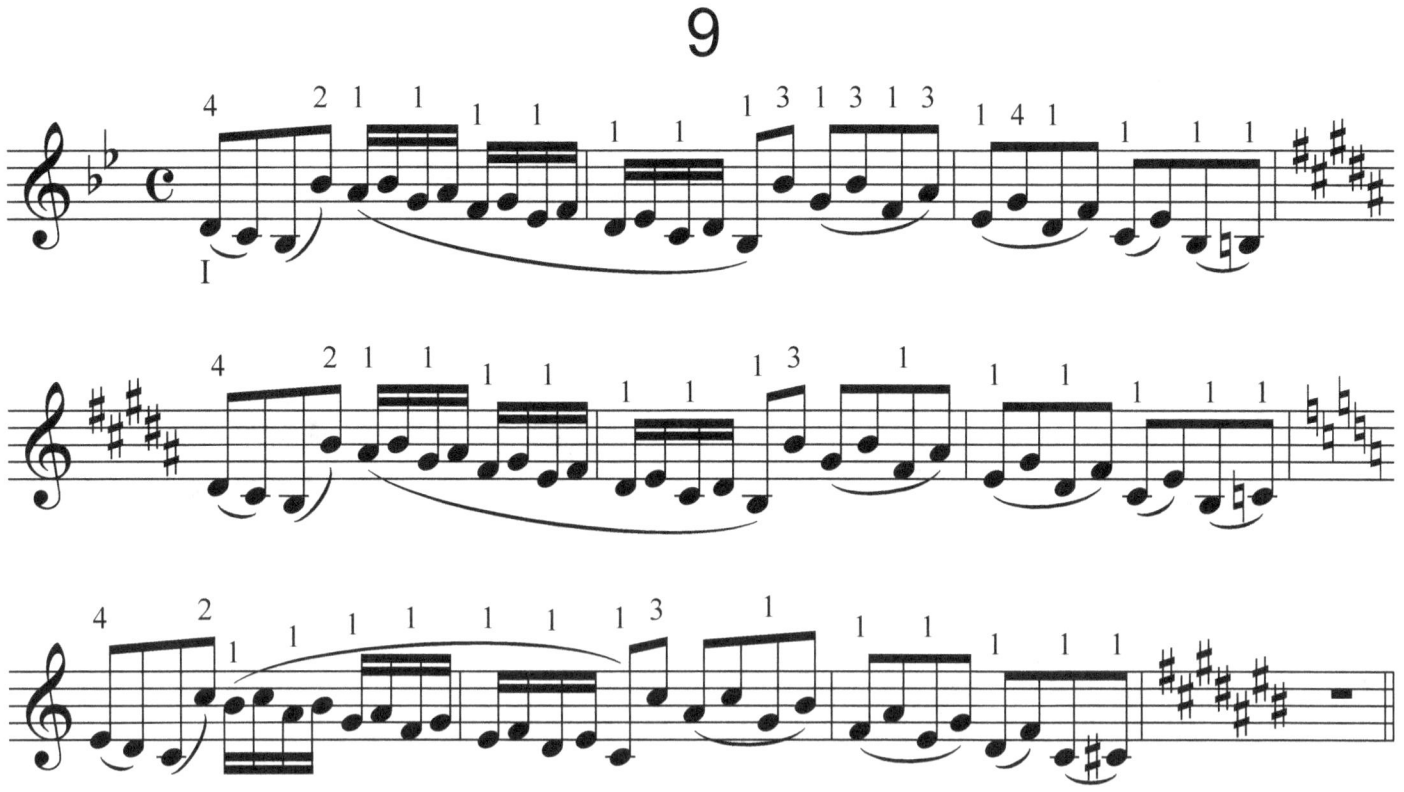

Continue playing the pattern and moving up the fingerboard in half steps, changing the key each time the pattern is played. When the exercise reaches fifth position, substitute 3rd finger for 4th finger.

10

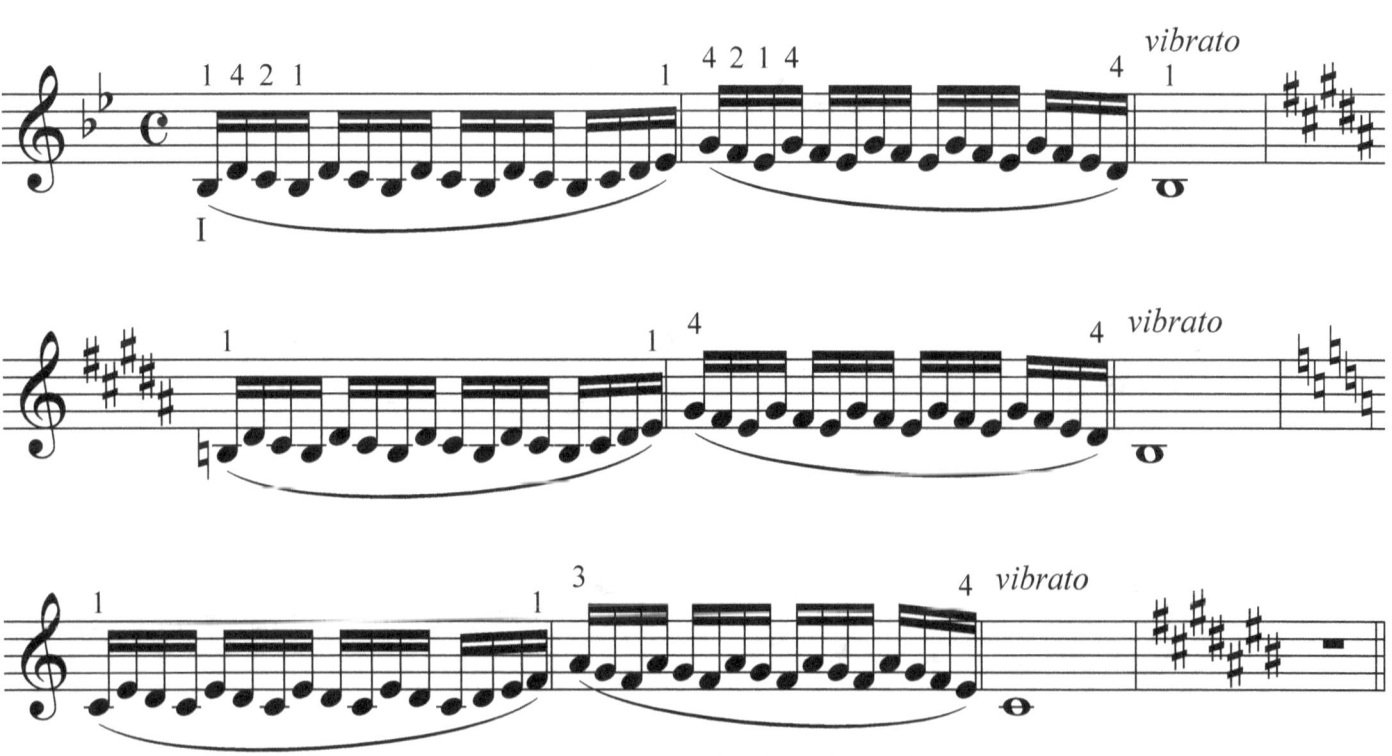

Continue playing the pattern and moving up the fingerboard in half steps, changing the key each time the pattern is played. When the exercise reaches fifth position, substitute 3rd finger for 4th finger.

©2018 C. Harvey Publications All Rights Reserved.

Warm-Ups for the Advanced Cellist, Book One

11

Continue playing the pattern and moving up the fingerboard in half steps, changing the key each time the pattern is played. When the exercise reaches fifth position, substitute 3rd finger for 4th finger.

12

Continue playing the pattern and moving up the fingerboard in half steps, changing the key each time the pattern is played. When the exercise reaches fifth position, substitute 3rd finger for 4th finger.

©2018 C. Harvey Publications All Rights Reserved.

Warm-Ups for the Advanced Cellist, Book One

13

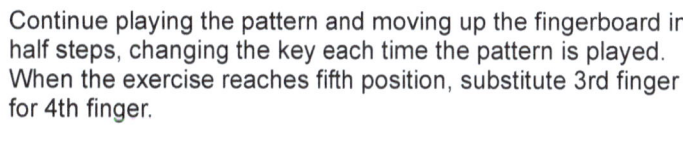

Continue playing the pattern and moving up the fingerboard in half steps, changing the key each time the pattern is played. When the exercise reaches fifth position, substitute 3rd finger for 4th finger.

14

Continue playing the pattern and moving up the fingerboard in half steps, changing the key each time the pattern is played. When the exercise reaches fifth position, substitute 3rd finger for 4th finger.

©2018 C. Harvey Publications All Rights Reserved.

15

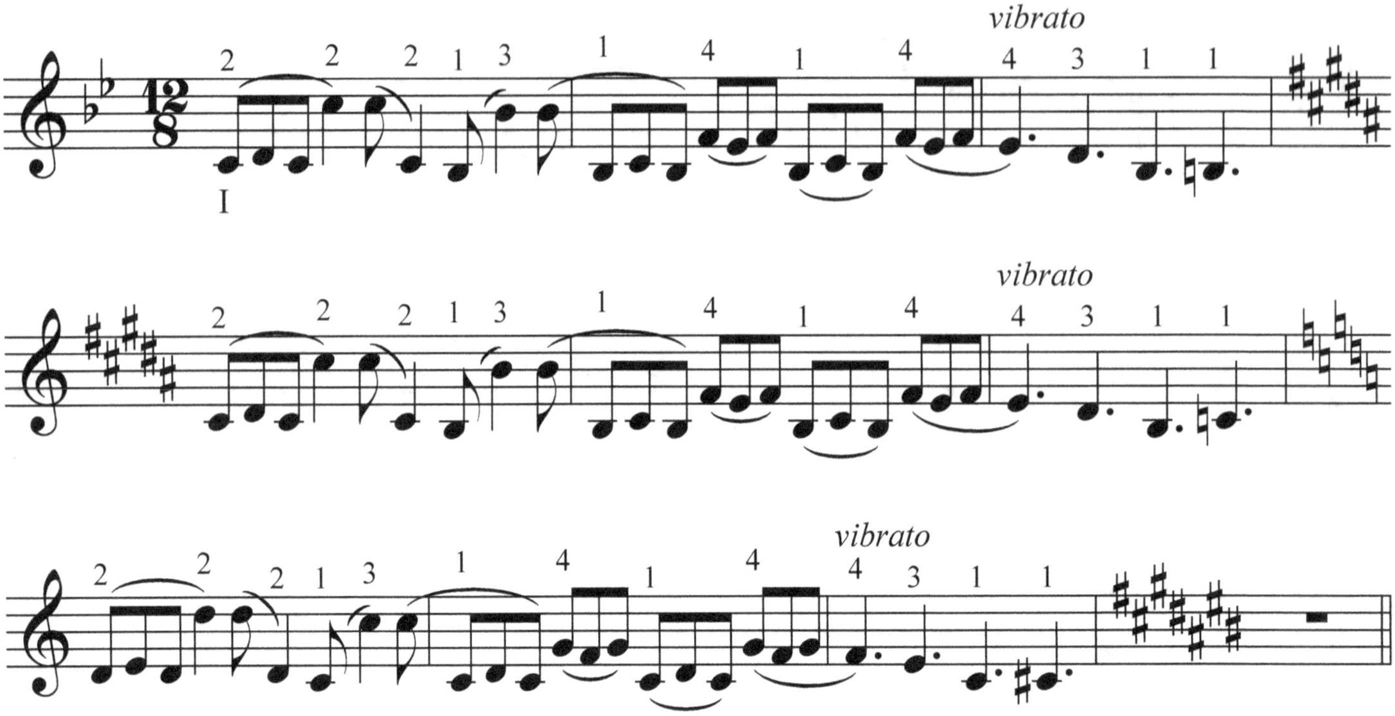

Continue playing the pattern and moving up the fingerboard in half steps, changing the key each time the pattern is played. When the exercise reaches fifth position, substitute 3rd finger for 4th finger.

16

Continue playing the pattern and moving up the fingerboard in half steps, changing the key each time the pattern is played. When the exercise reaches fifth position, substitute 3rd finger for 4th finger.

Warm-Ups for the Advanced Cellist, Book One

17

Continue playing the pattern and moving up the fingerboard in half steps, changing the key each time the pattern is played. When the exercise reaches fifth position, substitute 3rd finger for 4th finger.

18

Continue playing the pattern and moving up the fingerboard in half steps, changing the key each time the pattern is played. When the exercise reaches fifth position, substitute 3rd finger for 4th finger.

©2018 C. Harvey Publications All Rights Reserved.

19

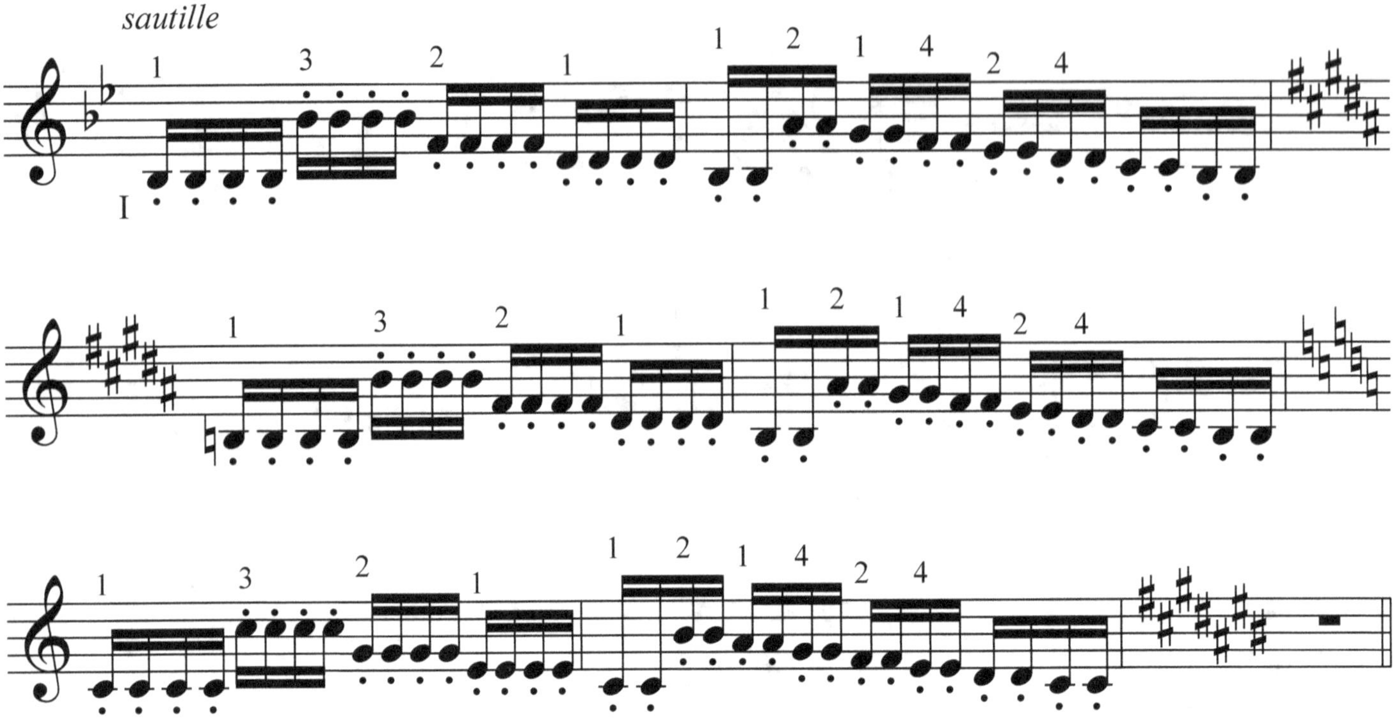
sautille

Continue playing the pattern and moving up the fingerboard in half steps, changing the key each time the pattern is played. When the exercise reaches fifth position, substitute 3rd finger for 4th finger.

20

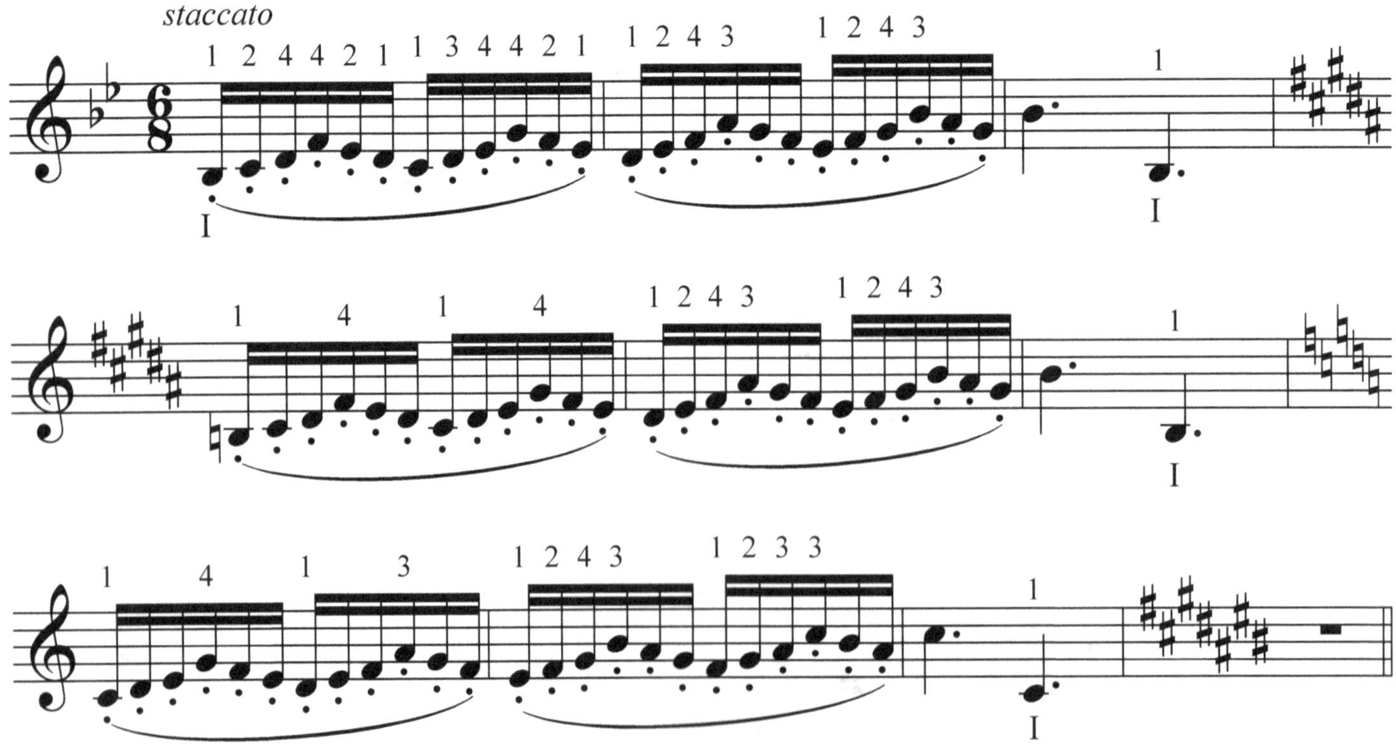
staccato

Continue playing the pattern and moving up the fingerboard in half steps, changing the key each time the pattern is played. When the exercise reaches fifth position, substitute 3rd finger for 4th finger.

©2018 C. Harvey Publications All Rights Reserved.

Warm-Ups for the Advanced Cellist, Book One

21

Continue playing the pattern and moving up the fingerboard in half steps, changing the key each time the pattern is played. When the exercise reaches fifth position, substitute 3rd finger for 4th finger.

22

Continue playing the pattern and moving up the fingerboard in half steps, changing the key each time the pattern is played. When the exercise reaches fifth position, substitute 3rd finger for 4th finger.

©2018 C. Harvey Publications All Rights Reserved.

23

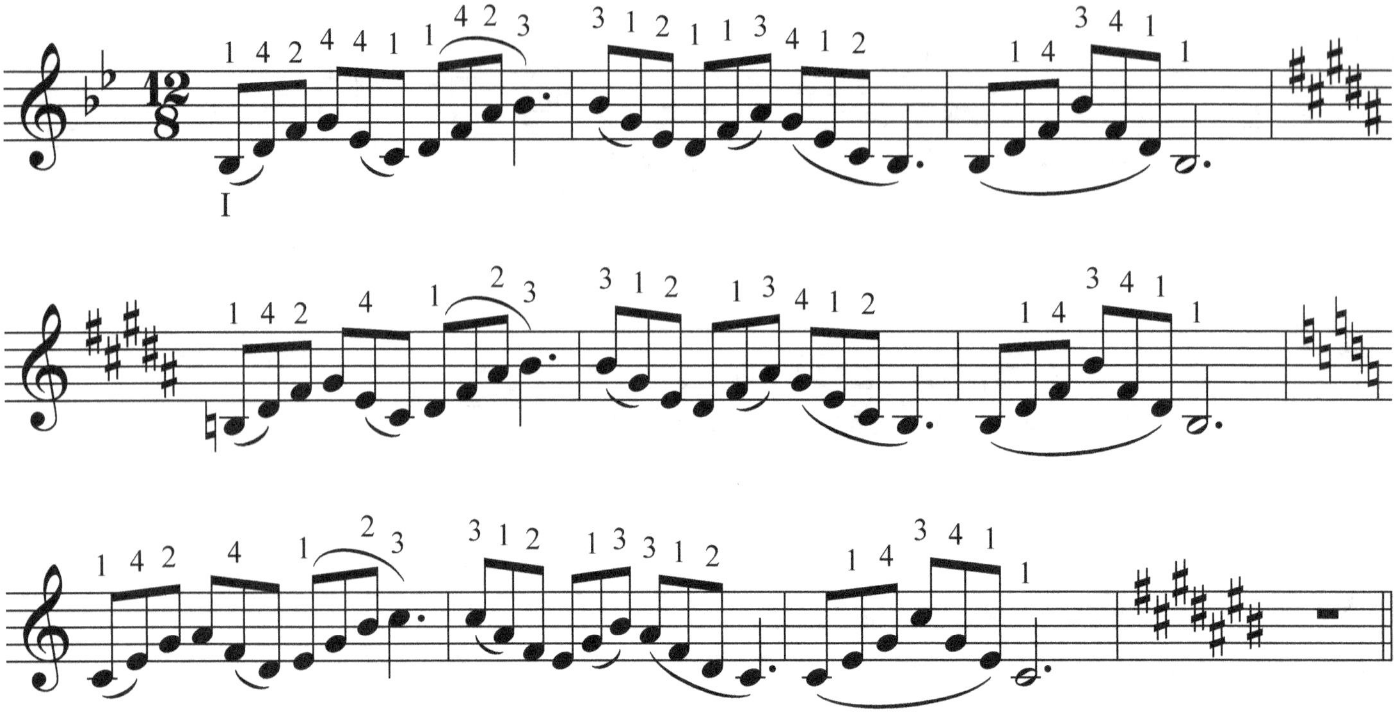

Continue playing the pattern and moving up the fingerboard in half steps, changing the key each time the pattern is played. When the exercise reaches fifth position, substitute 3rd finger for 4th finger.

24

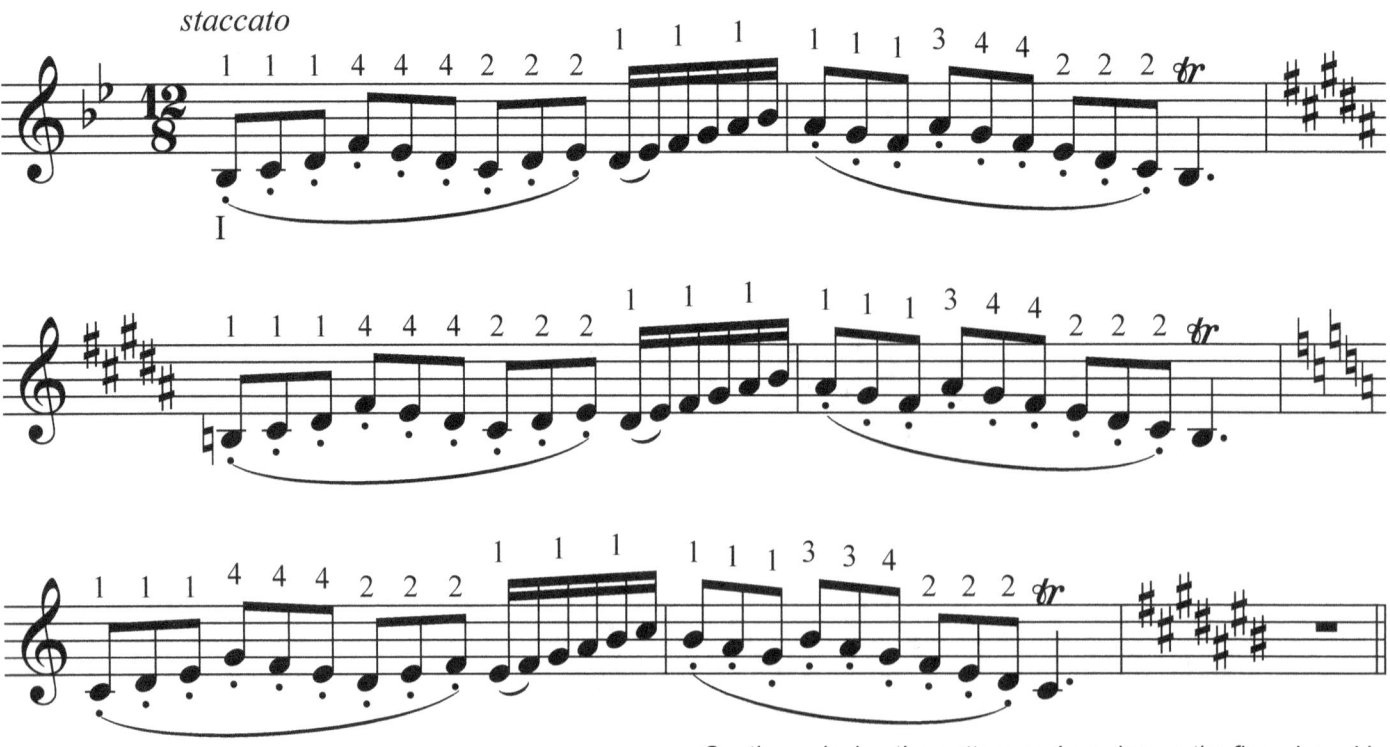

Continue playing the pattern and moving up the fingerboard in half steps, changing the key each time the pattern is played. When the exercise reaches fifth position, substitute 3rd finger for 4th finger.

©2018 C. Harvey Publications All Rights Reserved.

Warm-Ups for the Advanced Cellist, Book One

Thumb Position

25

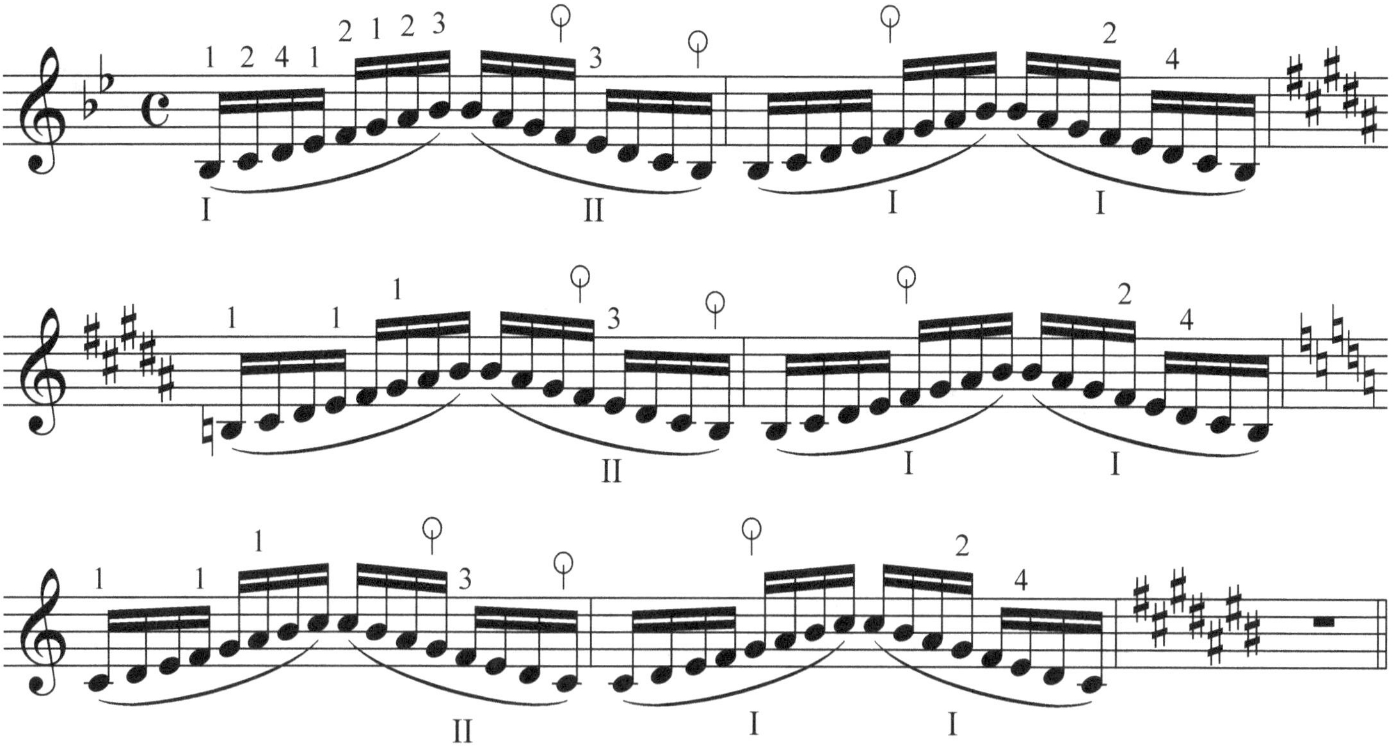

Continue playing the pattern and moving up the fingerboard in half steps, changing the key each time the pattern is played. When the exercise reaches fifth position, substitute 3rd finger for 4th finger.

26

Continue playing the pattern and moving up the fingerboard in half steps, changing the key each time the pattern is played. When the exercise reaches fifth position, substitute 3rd finger for 4th finger.

©2018 C. Harvey Publications All Rights Reserved.

27

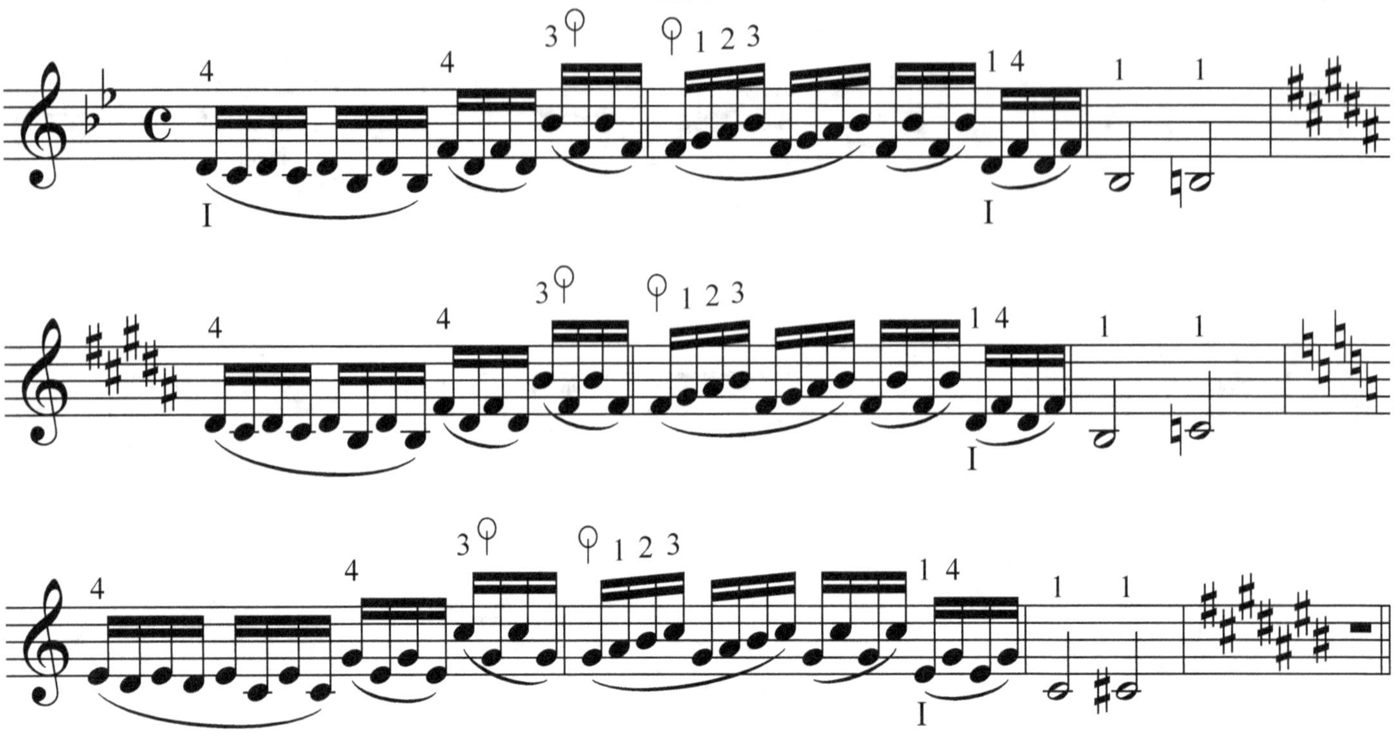

Continue playing the pattern and moving up the fingerboard in half steps, changing the key each time the pattern is played. When the exercise reaches fifth position, substitute 3rd finger for 4th finger.

28

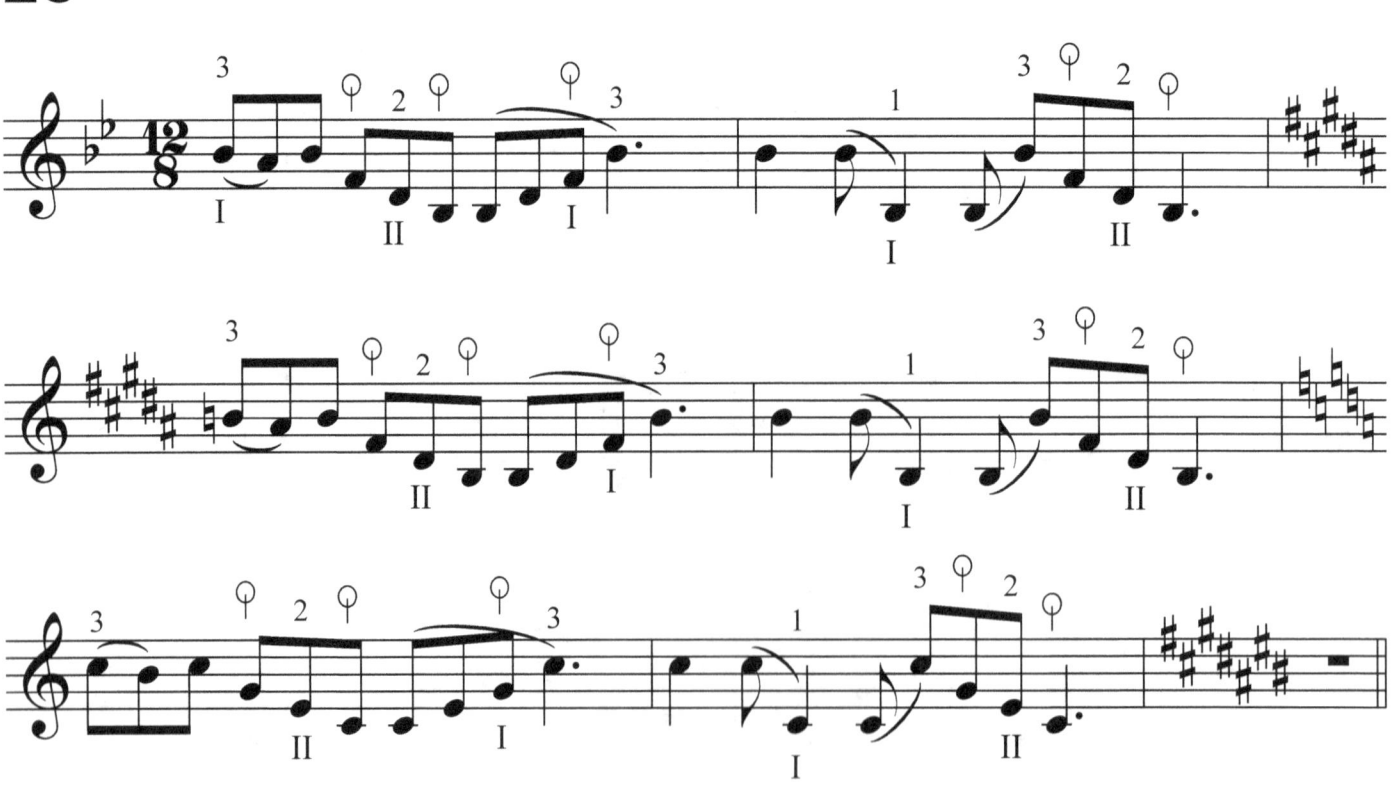

Continue playing the pattern and moving up the fingerboard in half steps, changing the key each time the pattern is played.

©2018 C. Harvey Publications All Rights Reserved.

Warm-Ups for the Advanced Cellist, Book One

29

spiccato

spiccato

spiccato

Continue playing the pattern and moving up the fingerboard in half steps, changing the key each time the pattern is played.

30

staccato

Continue playing the pattern and moving up the fingerboard in half steps, changing the key each time the pattern is played. When the exercise reaches fifth position, substitute 3rd finger for 4th finger.

©2018 C. Harvey Publications All Rights Reserved.

31

Continue playing the pattern and moving up the fingerboard in half steps, changing the key each time the pattern is played. When the exercise reaches fifth position, substitute 3rd finger for 4th finger.

32

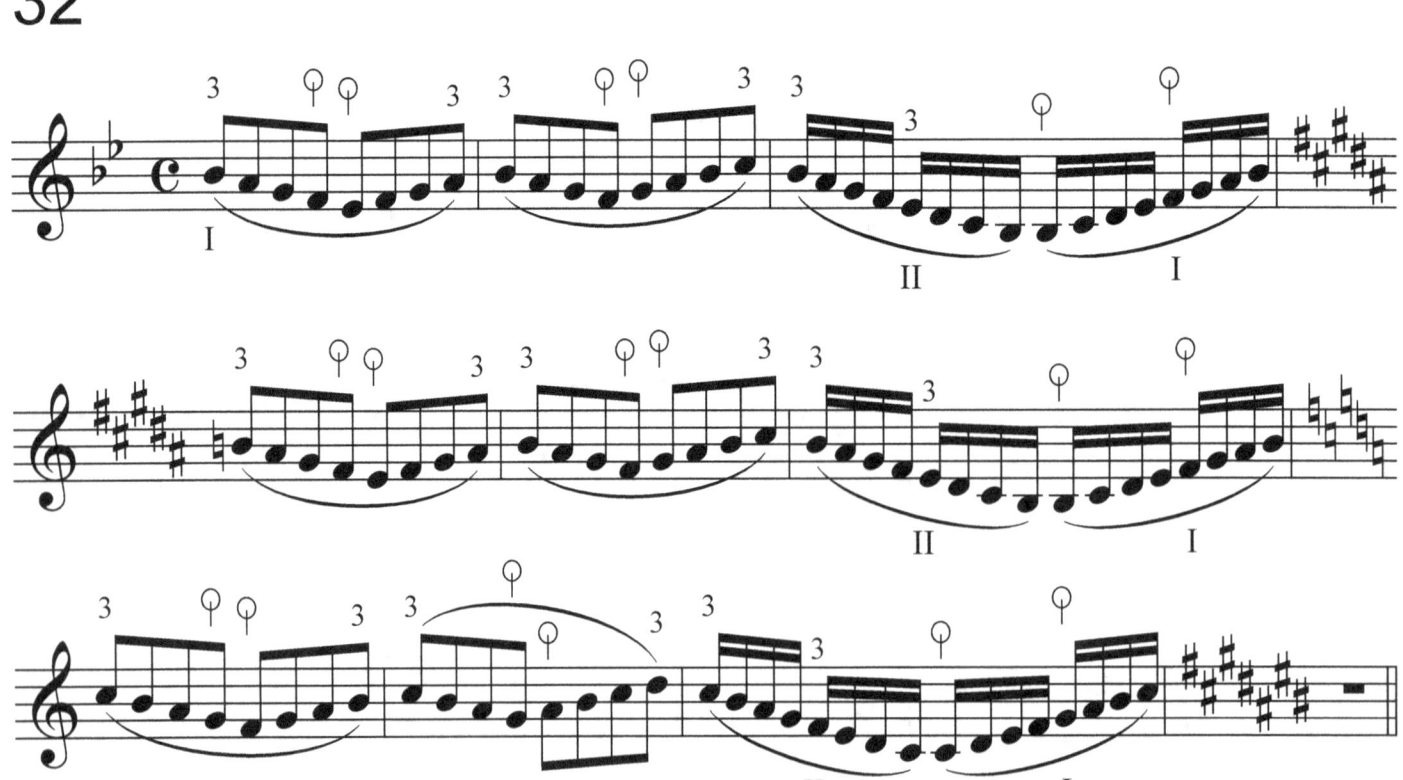

Continue playing the pattern and moving up the fingerboard in half steps, changing the key each time the pattern is played.

Warm-Ups for the Advanced Cellist, Book One

33

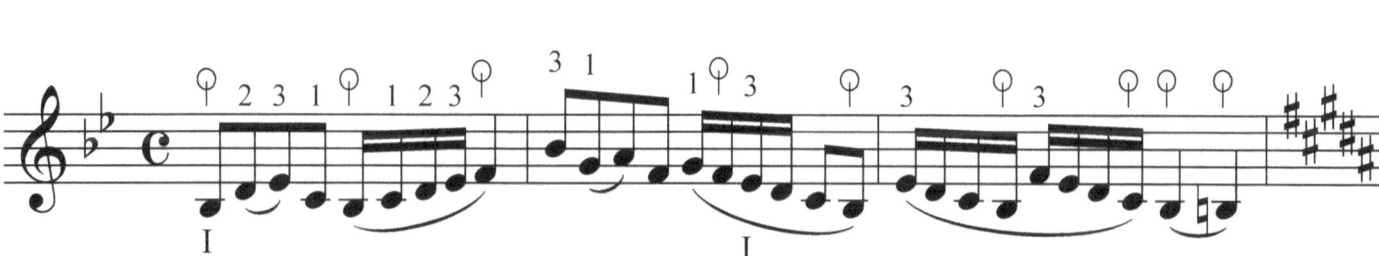

Continue playing the pattern and moving up the fingerboard in
half steps, changing the key each time the pattern is played.

34

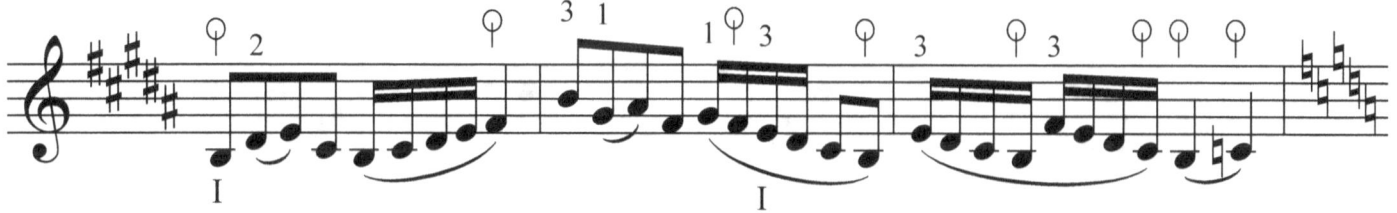

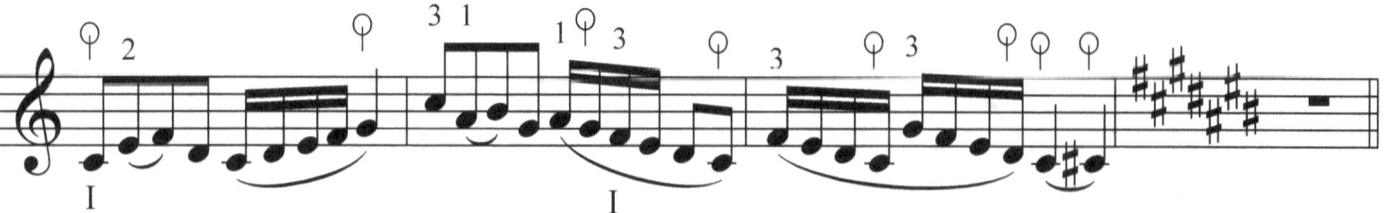

Continue playing the pattern and moving up the fingerboard in
half steps, changing the key each time the pattern is played.

©2018 C. Harvey Publications All Rights Reserved.

35

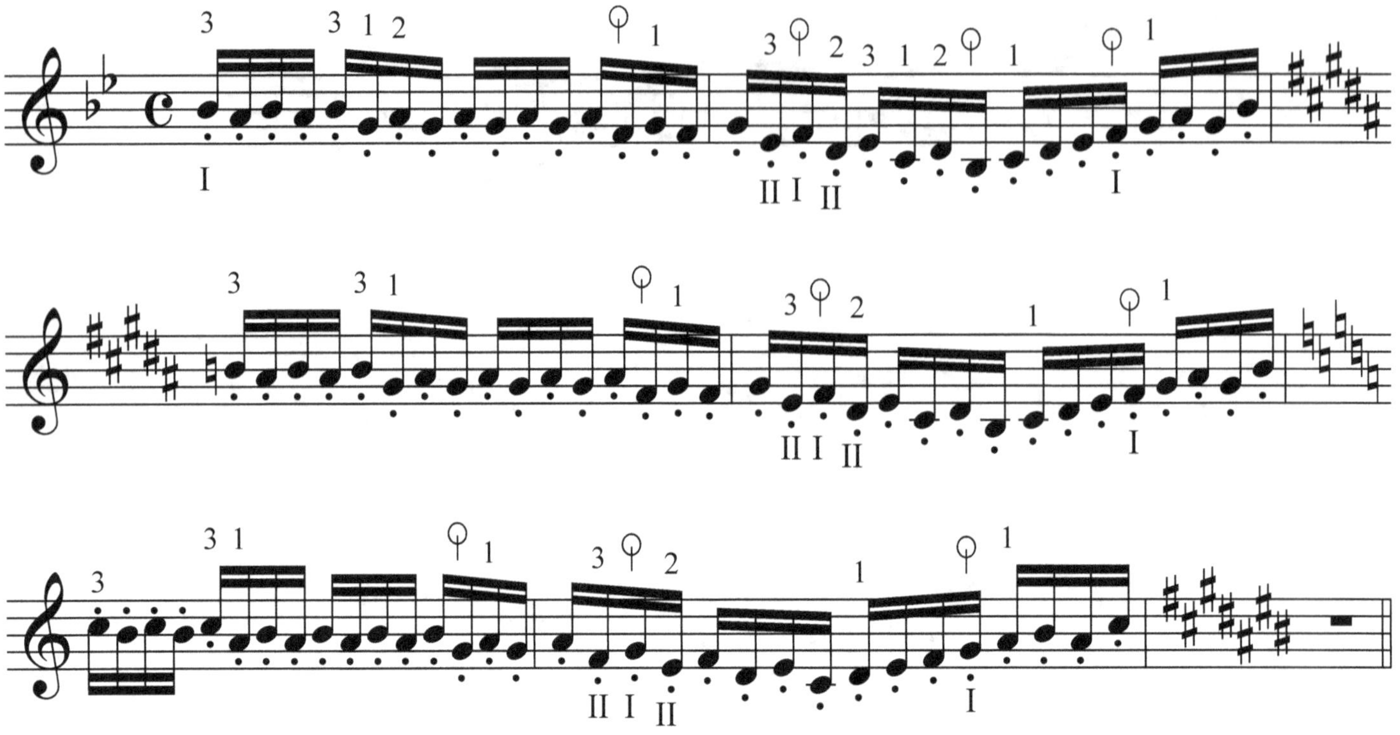

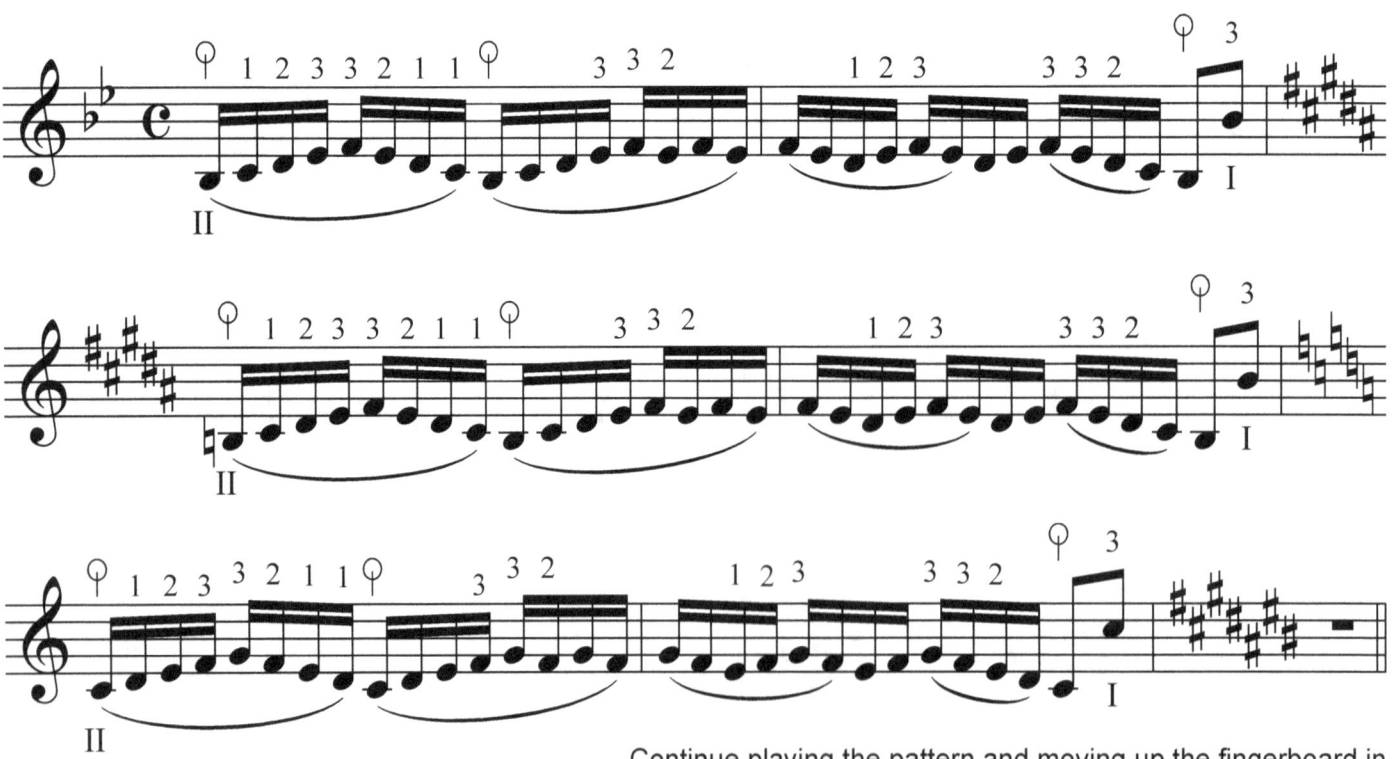

Continue playing the pattern and moving up the fingerboard in half steps, changing the key each time the pattern is played.

36

Continue playing the pattern and moving up the fingerboard in half steps, changing the key each time the pattern is played.

©2018 C. Harvey Publications All Rights Reserved.

Warm-Ups for the Advanced Cellist, Book One

37

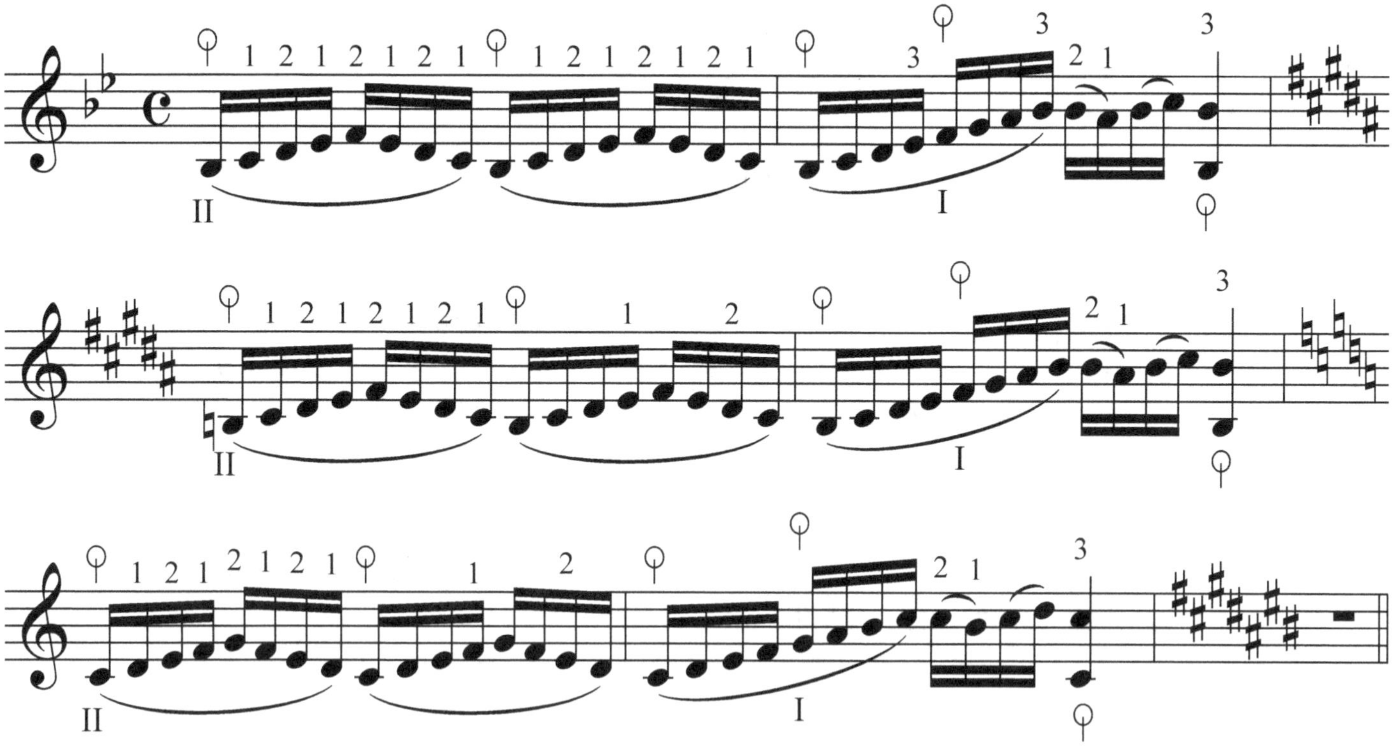

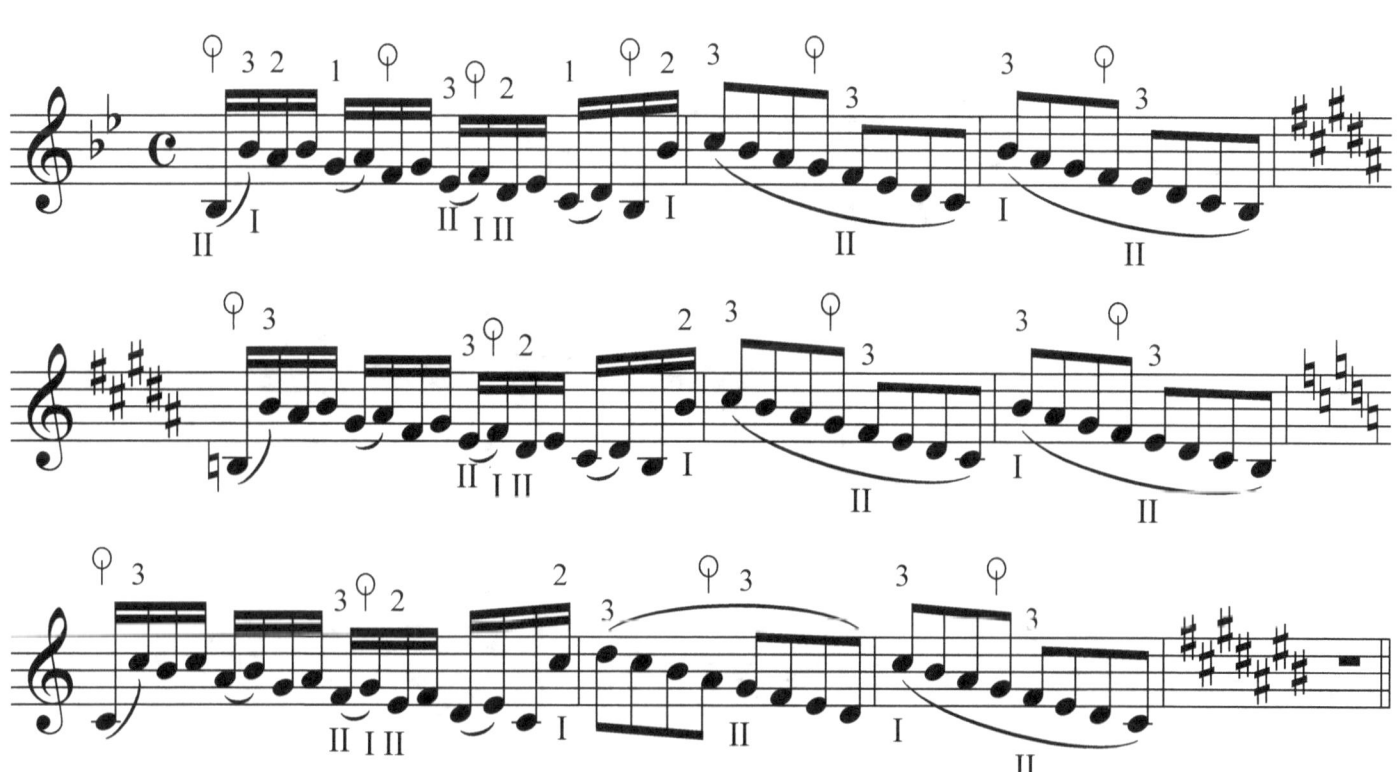

Continue playing the pattern and moving up the fingerboard in half steps, changing the key each time the pattern is played.

38

Continue playing the pattern and moving up the fingerboard in half steps, changing the key each time the pattern is played.

©2018 C. Harvey Publications All Rights Reserved.

39

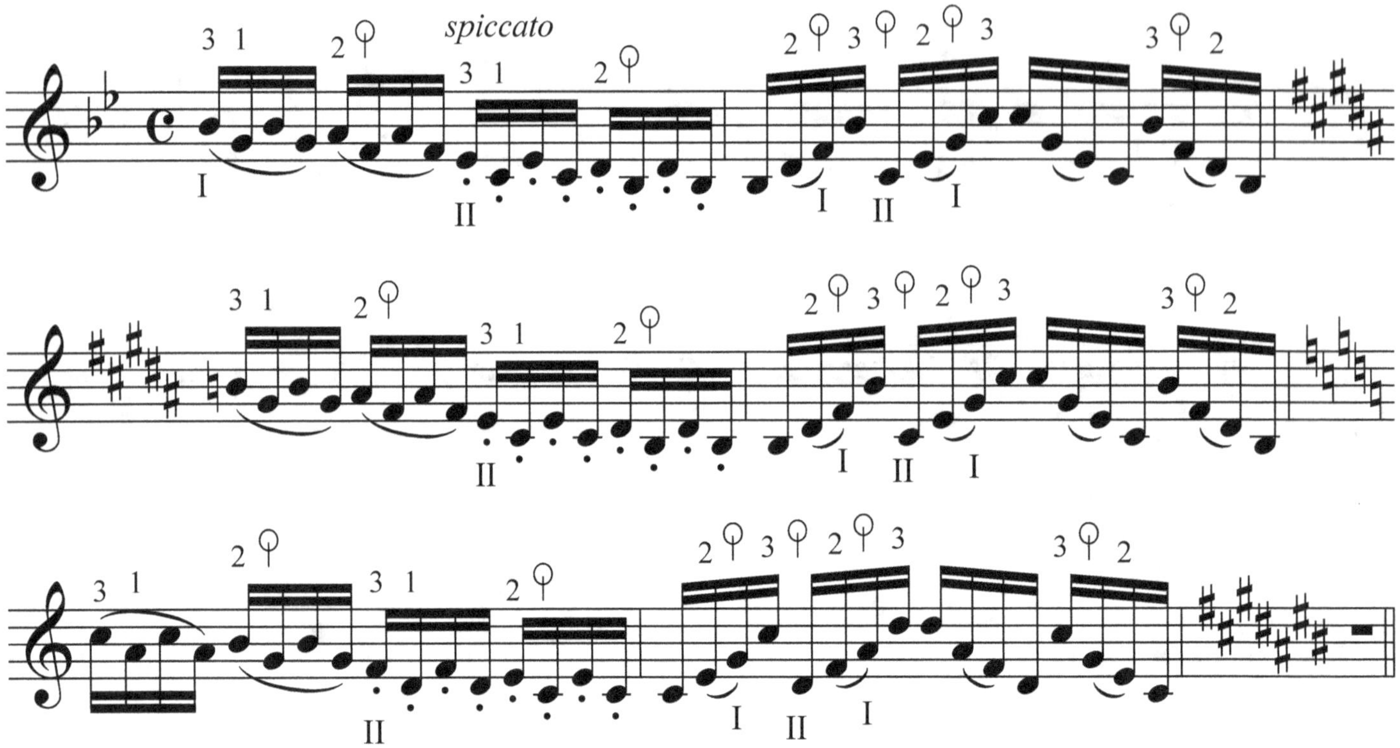

Continue playing the pattern and moving up the fingerboard in half steps, changing the key each time the pattern is played.

40

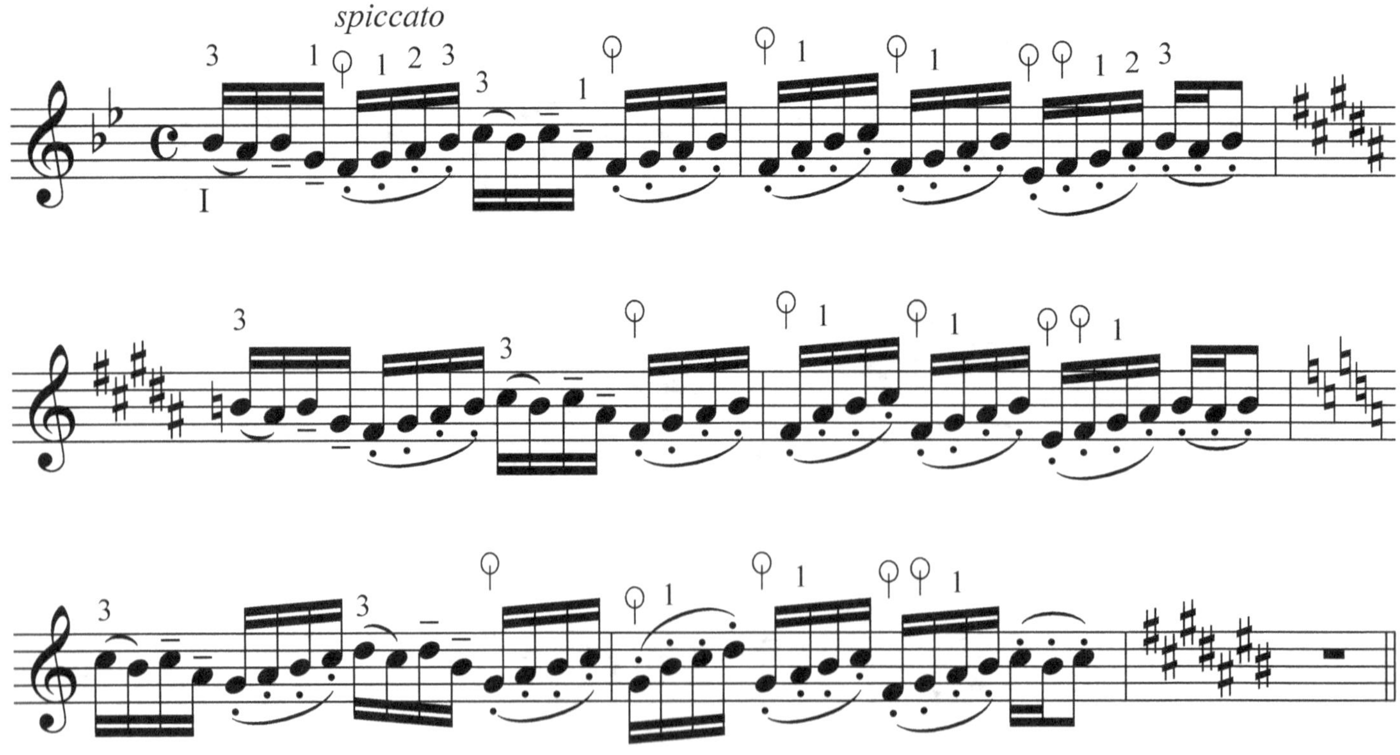

Continue playing the pattern and moving up the fingerboard in half steps, changing the key each time the pattern is played.

Warm-Ups for the Advanced Cellist, Book One 21

41

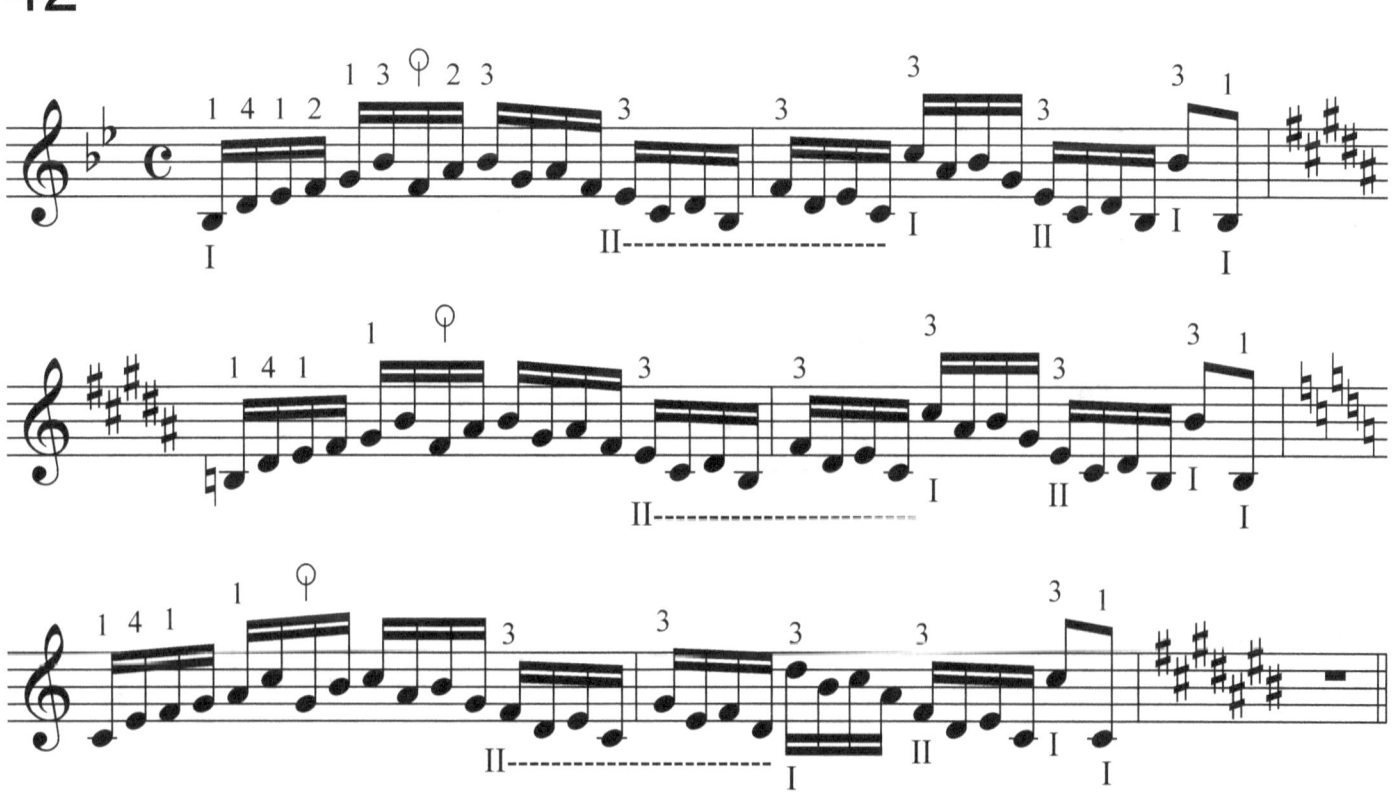

Continue playing the pattern and moving up the fingerboard in half steps, changing the key each time the pattern is played.

42

Continue playing the pattern and moving up the fingerboard in half steps, changing the key each time the pattern is played. When the exercise reaches fifth position, substitute 3rd finger for 4th finger.

©2018 C. Harvey Publications All Rights Reserved.

43

Continue playing the pattern and moving up the fingerboard in half steps, changing the key each time the pattern is played.

44

Continue playing the pattern and moving up the fingerboard in half steps, changing the key each time the pattern is played.

©2018 C. Harvey Publications All Rights Reserved.

Warm-Ups for the Advanced Cellist, Book One

45

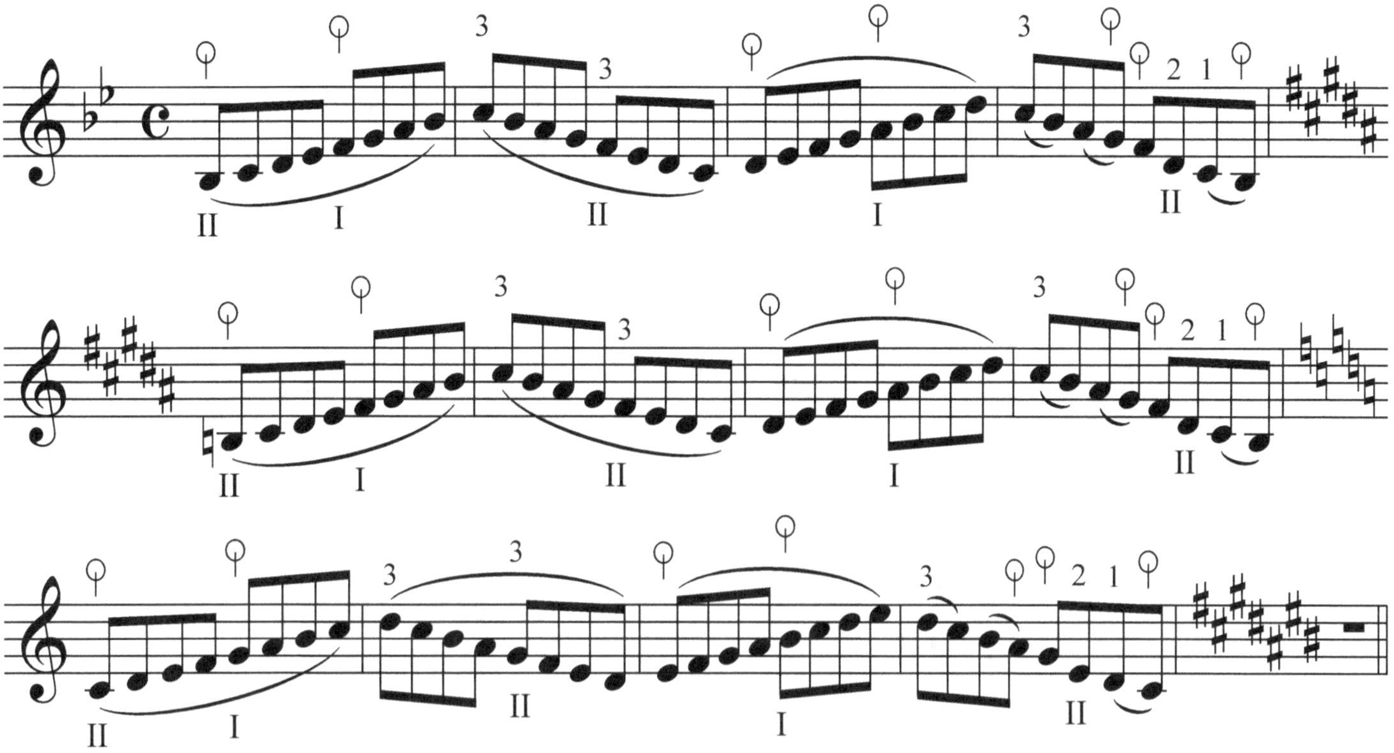

Continue playing the pattern and moving up the fingerboard in half steps, changing the key each time the pattern is played.

46

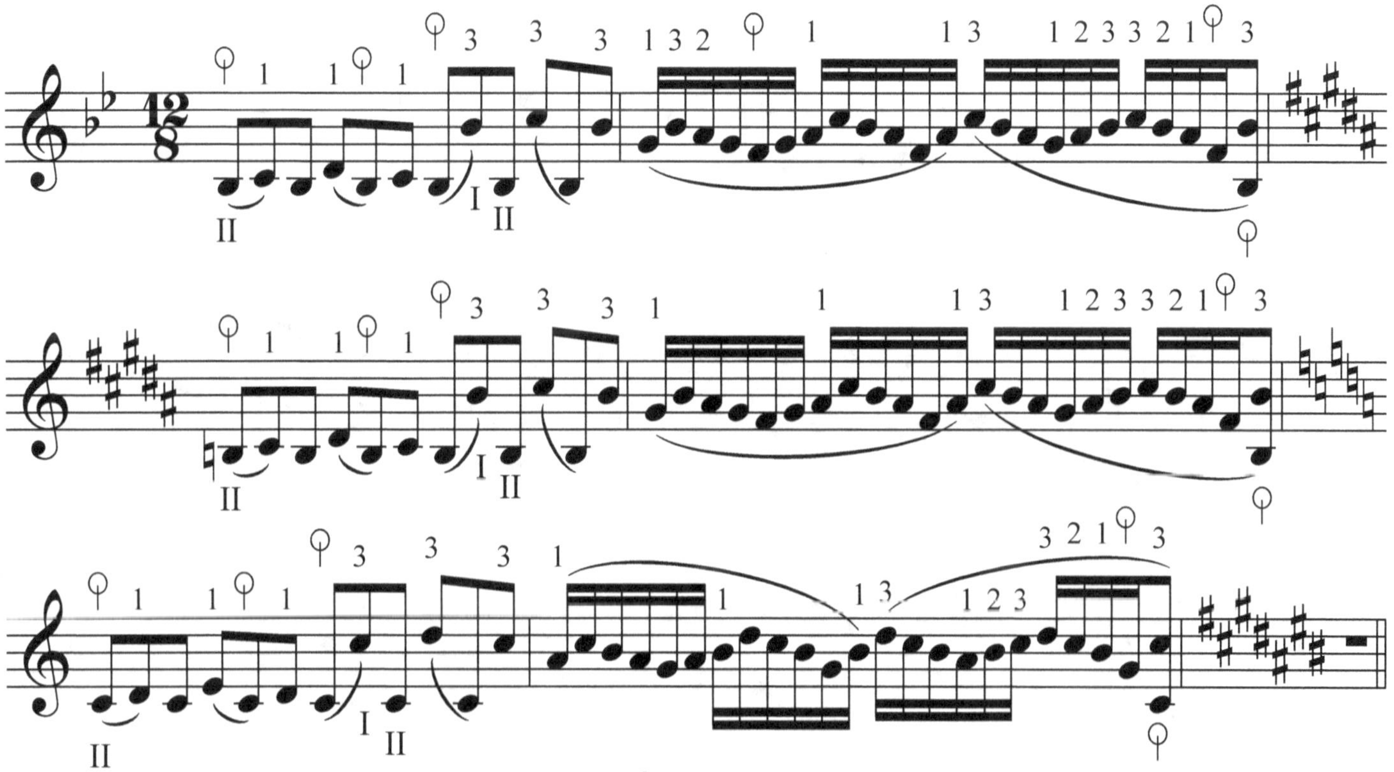

Continue playing the pattern and moving up the fingerboard in half steps, changing the key each time the pattern is played.

©2018 C. Harvey Publications All Rights Reserved.

47

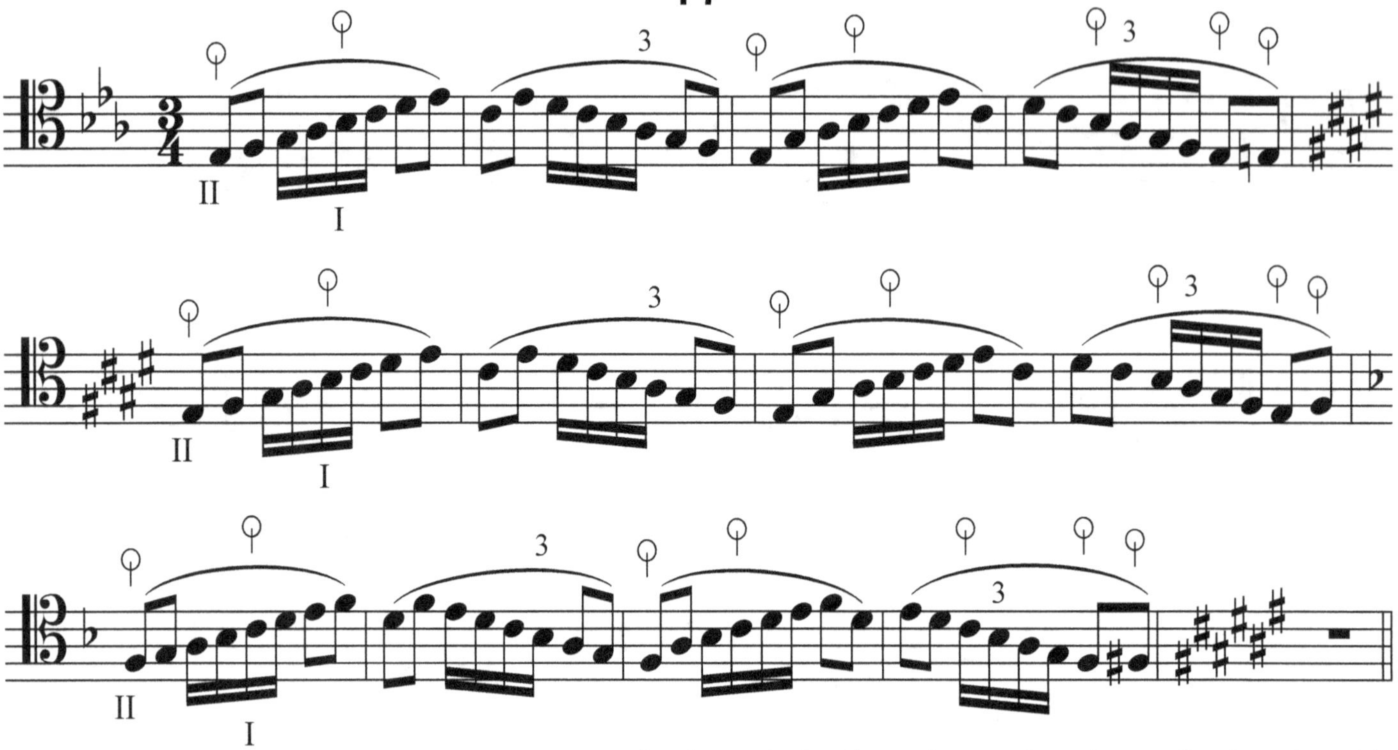

Continue playing the pattern and moving up the fingerboard in half steps, changing the key each time the pattern is played.

48

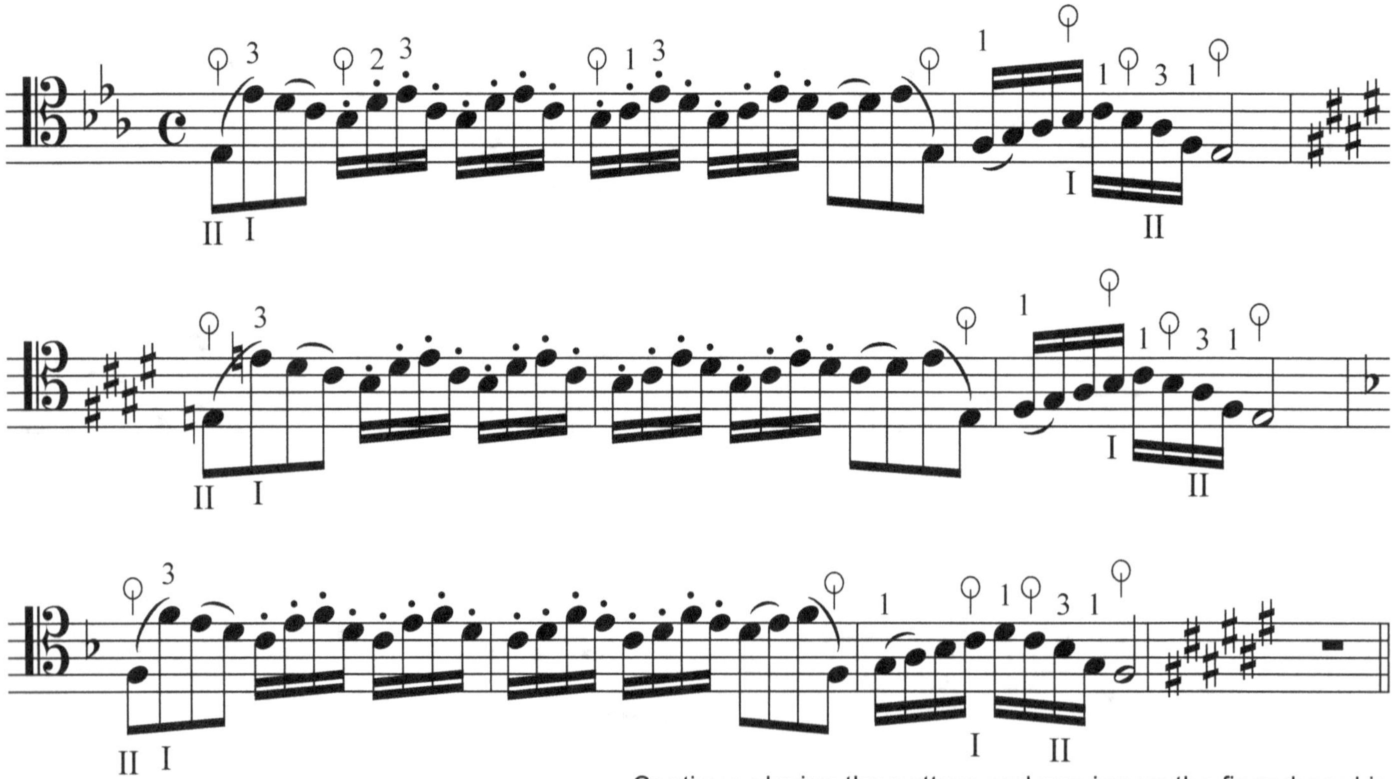

Continue playing the pattern and moving up the fingerboard in half steps, changing the key each time the pattern is played.

Warm-Ups for the Advanced Cellist, Book One

Octaves

49

Continue playing the pattern and moving up the fingerboard in half steps, changing the key each time the pattern is played.

50

Continue playing the pattern and moving up the fingerboard in half steps, changing the key each time the pattern is played.

©2018 C. Harvey Publications All Rights Reserved.

51

Continue playing the pattern and moving up the fingerboard in half steps, changing the key each time the pattern is played.

52

Continue playing the pattern and moving up the fingerboard in half steps, changing the key each time the pattern is played.

©2018 C. Harvey Publications All Rights Reserved.

Warm-Ups for the Advanced Cellist, Book One
27

53

Continue playing the pattern and moving up the fingerboard in half steps, changing the key each time the pattern is played.

54

Continue playing the pattern and moving up the fingerboard in half steps, changing the key each time the pattern is played.

©2018 C. Harvey Publications All Rights Reserved.

55

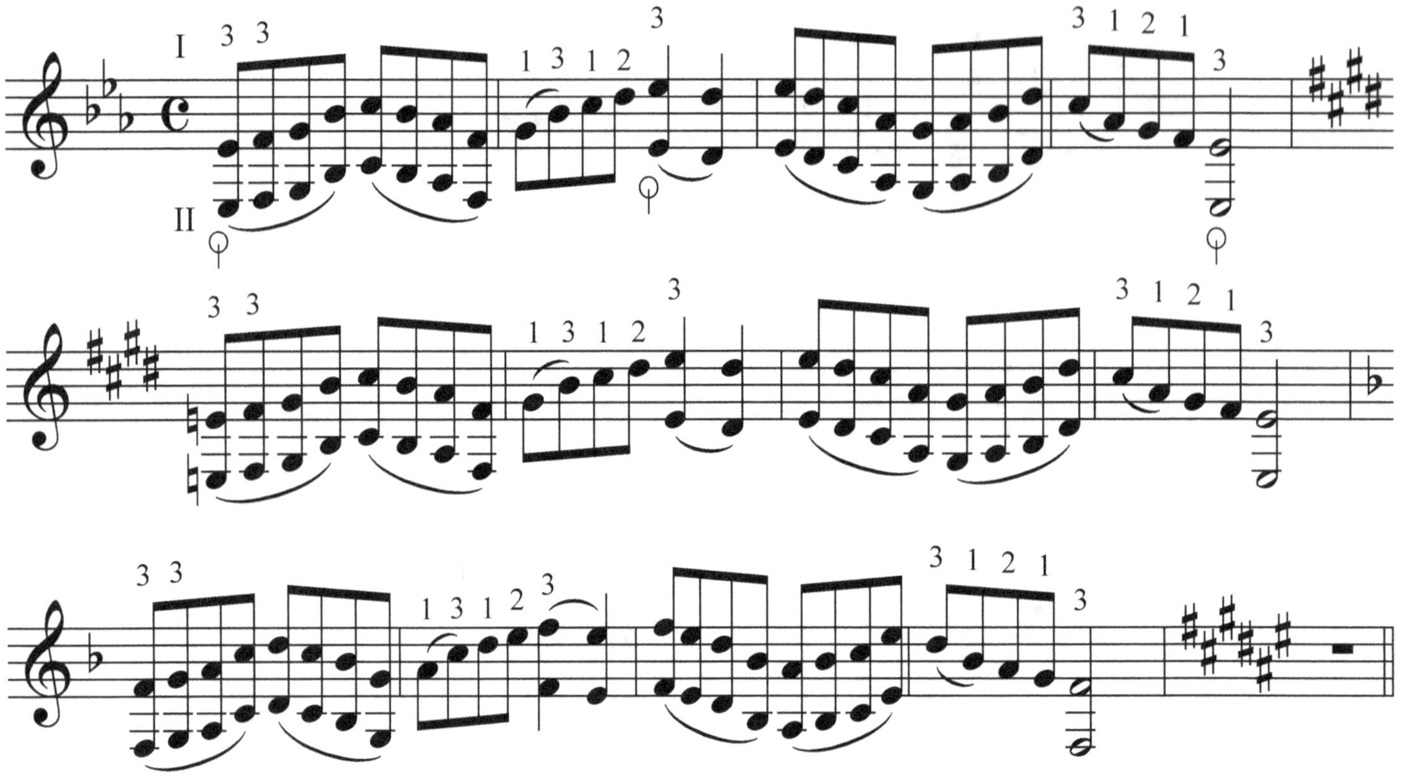

Continue playing the pattern and moving up the fingerboard in half steps, changing the key each time the pattern is played.

56

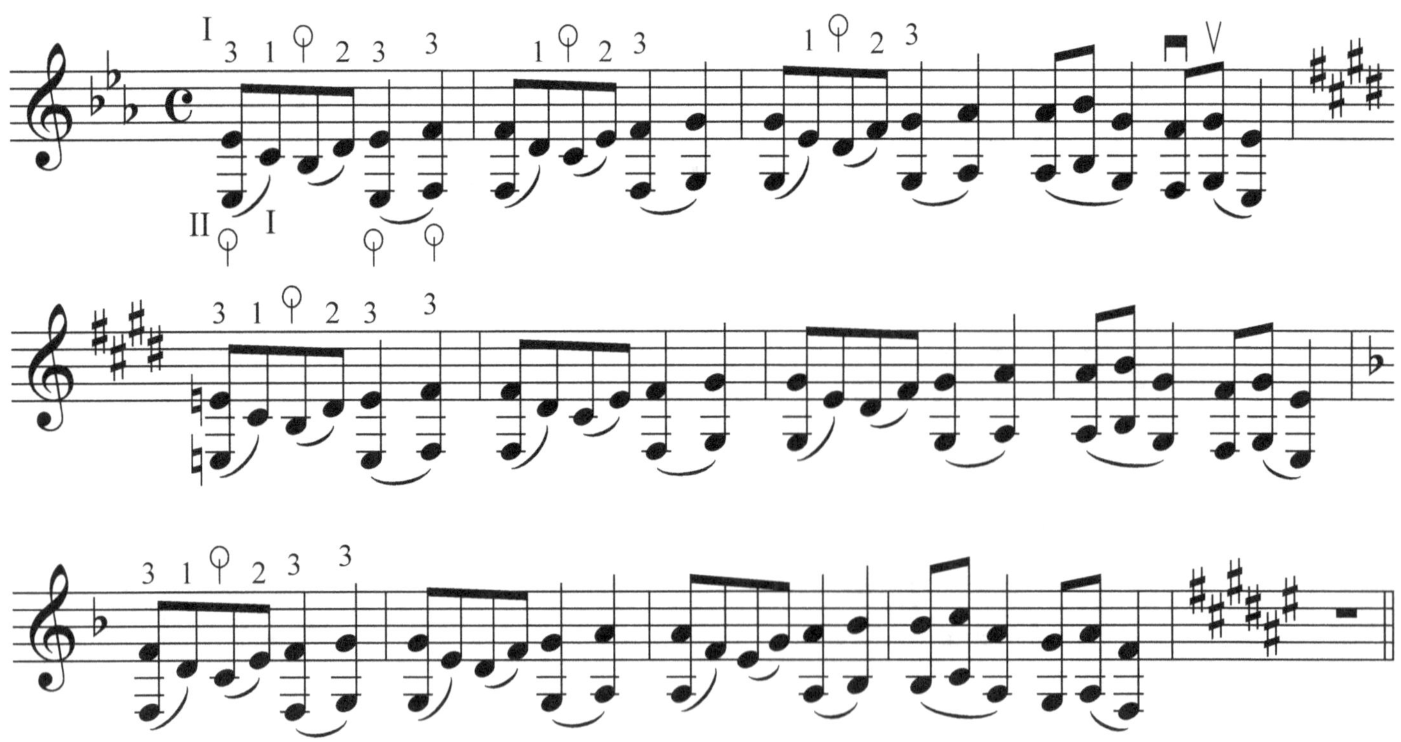

Continue playing the pattern and moving up the fingerboard in half steps, changing the key each time the pattern is played.

Warm-Ups for the Advanced Cellist, Book One

57

Continue playing the pattern and moving up the fingerboard in half steps, changing the key each time the pattern is played.

58

Continue playing the pattern and moving up the fingerboard in half steps, changing the key each time the pattern is played.

©2018 C. Harvey Publications All Rights Reserved.

59

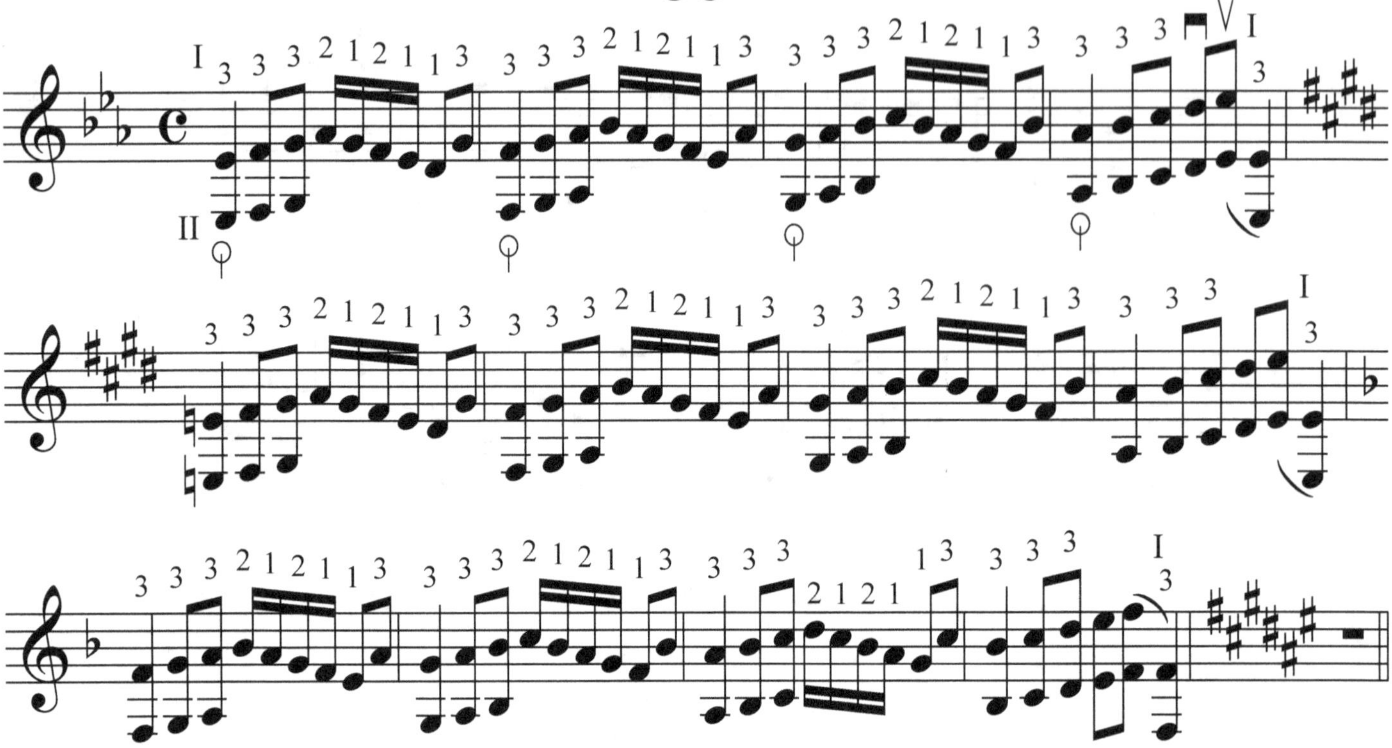

Continue playing the pattern and moving up the fingerboard in half steps, changing the key each time the pattern is played.

60

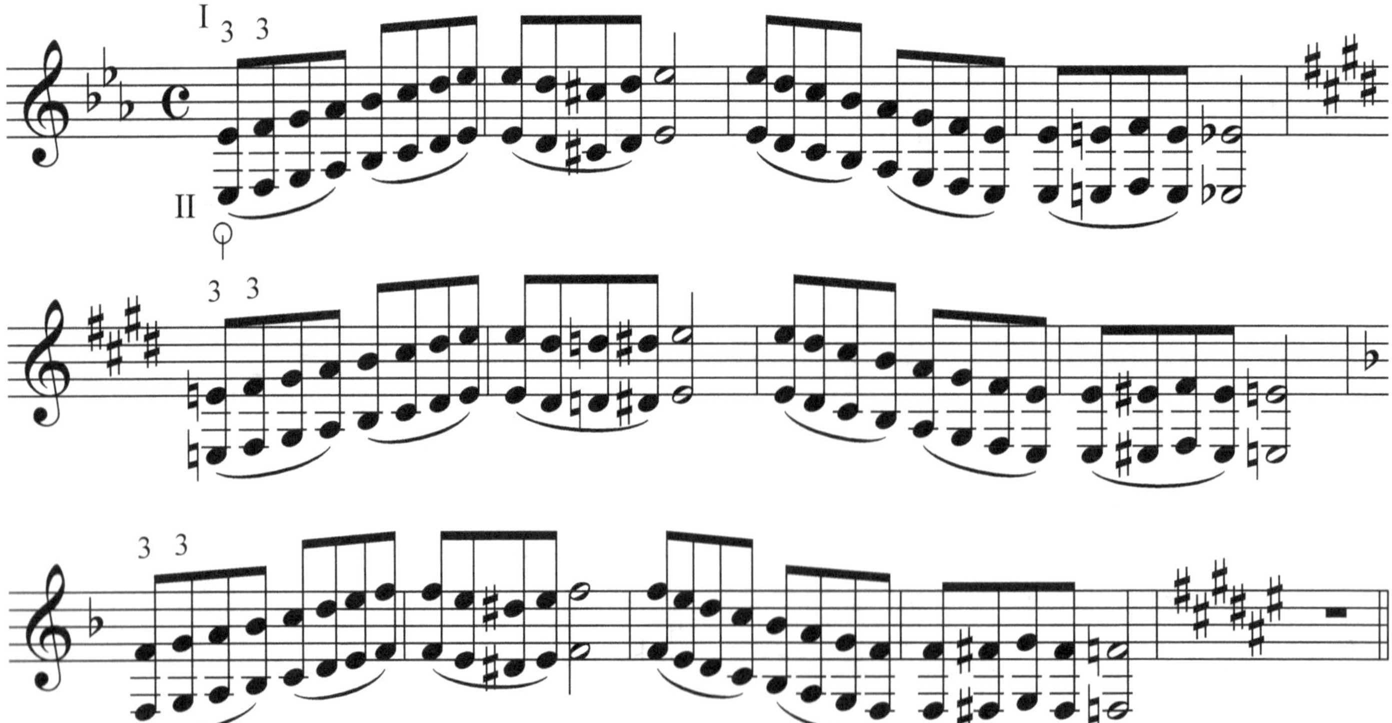

Continue playing the pattern and moving up the fingerboard in half steps, changing the key each time the pattern is played.

©2018 C. Harvey Publications All Rights Reserved.

Warm-Ups for the Advanced Cellist, Book One
31

61

Continue playing the pattern and moving up the fingerboard in half steps, changing the key each time the pattern is played.

62

Continue playing the pattern and moving up the fingerboard in half steps, changing the key each time the pattern is played.

©2018 C. Harvey Publications All Rights Reserved.

63

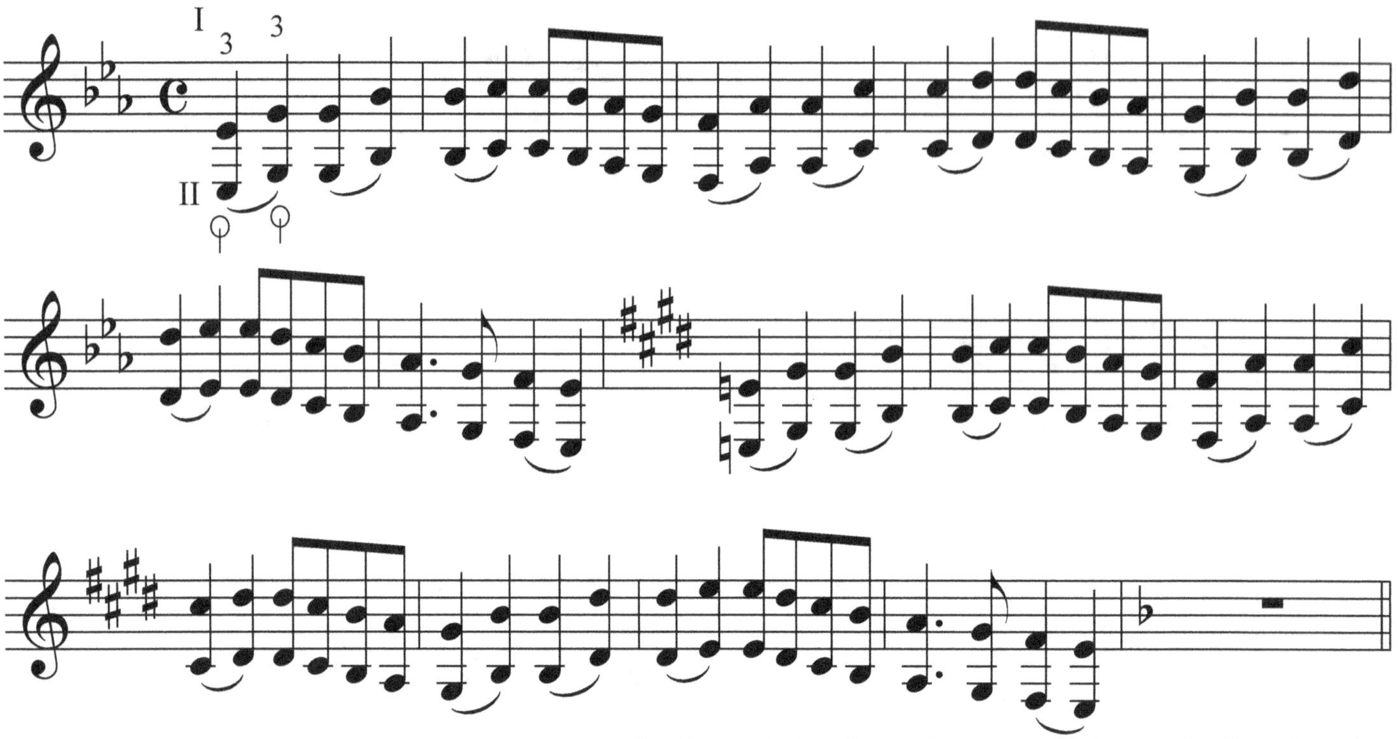

Continue playing the pattern and moving up the fingerboard in half steps, changing the key each time the pattern is played.

64

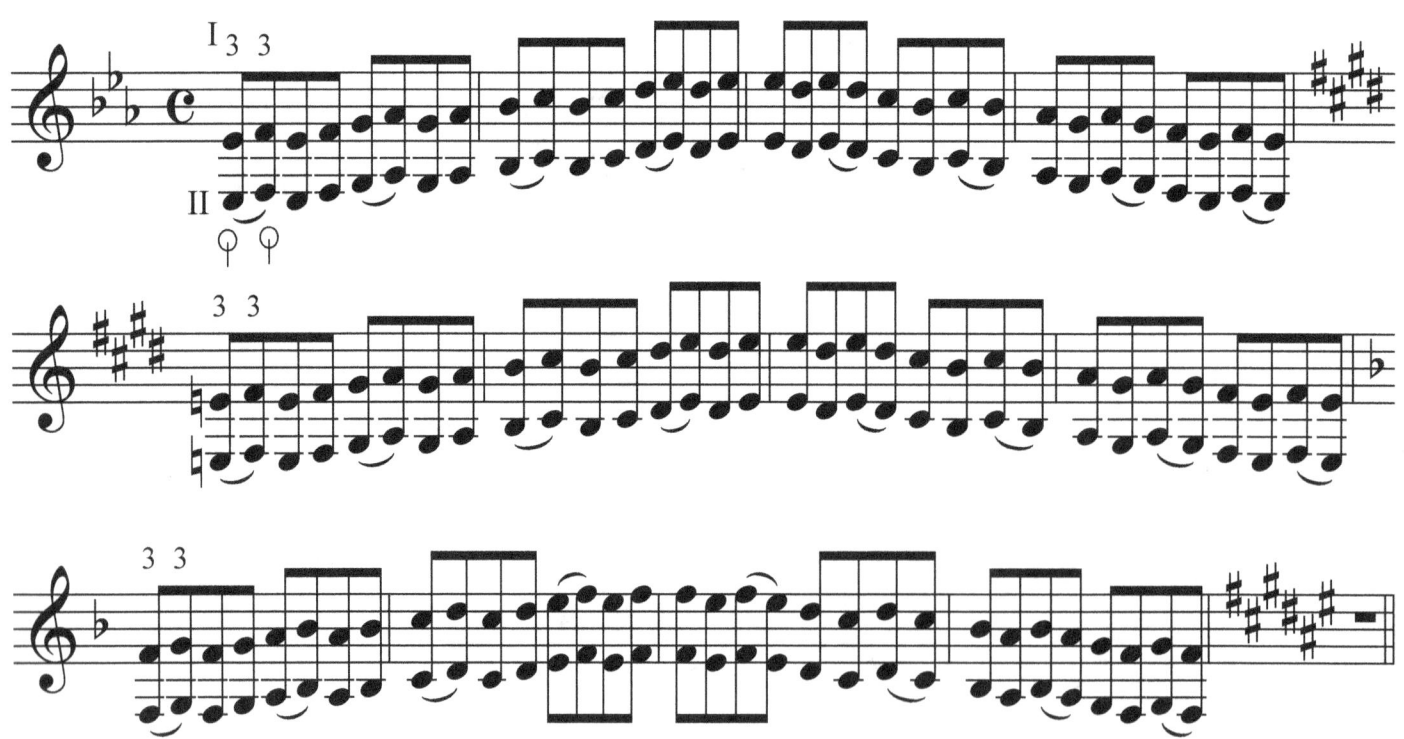

Continue playing the pattern and moving up the fingerboard in half steps, changing the key each time the pattern is played.

©2018 C. Harvey Publications All Rights Reserved.

Warm-Ups for the Advanced Cellist, Book One

65

Continue playing the pattern and moving up the fingerboard in half steps, changing the key each time the pattern is played.

66

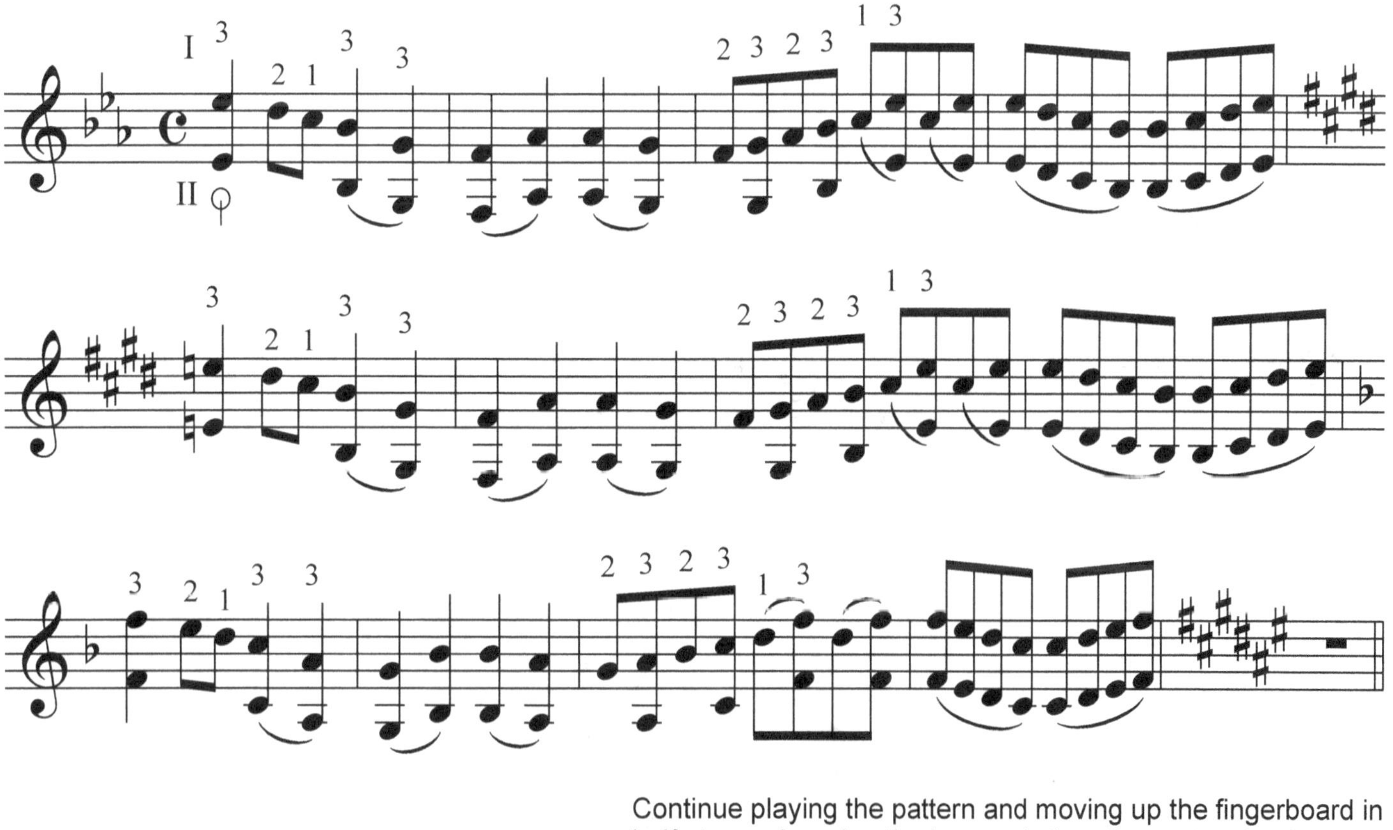

Continue playing the pattern and moving up the fingerboard in half steps, changing the key each time the pattern is played.

©2018 C. Harvey Publications All Rights Reserved.

67

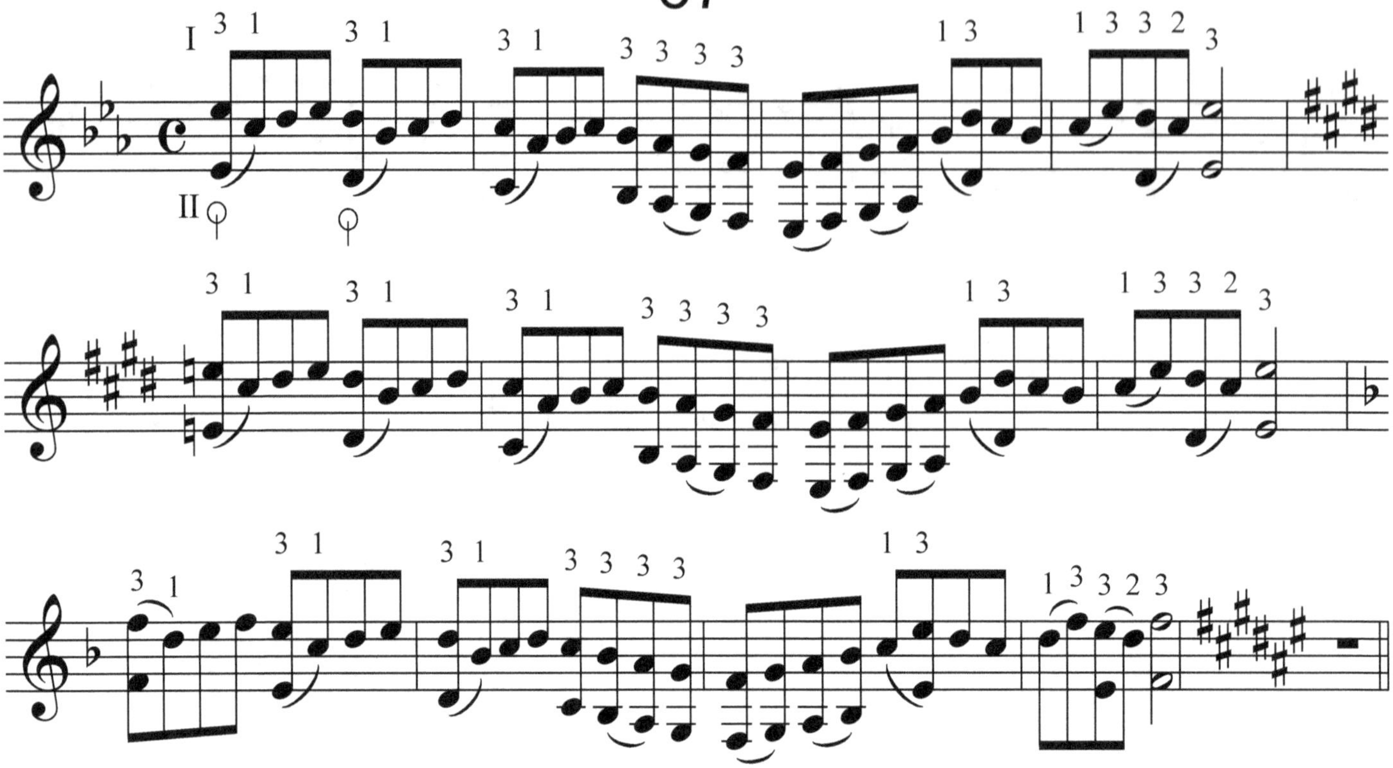

Continue playing the pattern and moving up the fingerboard in half steps, changing the key each time the pattern is played.

68

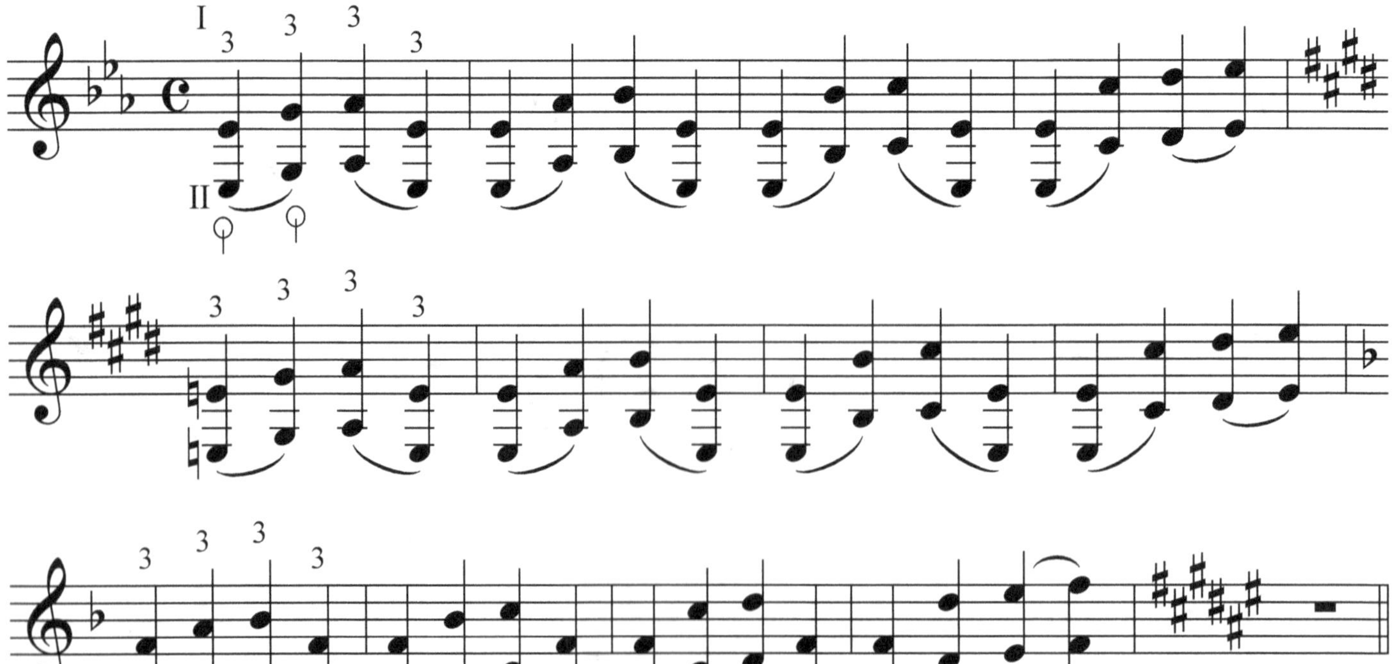

Continue playing the pattern and moving up the fingerboard in half steps, changing the key each time the pattern is played.

©2018 C. Harvey Publications All Rights Reserved.

Chromatics

69

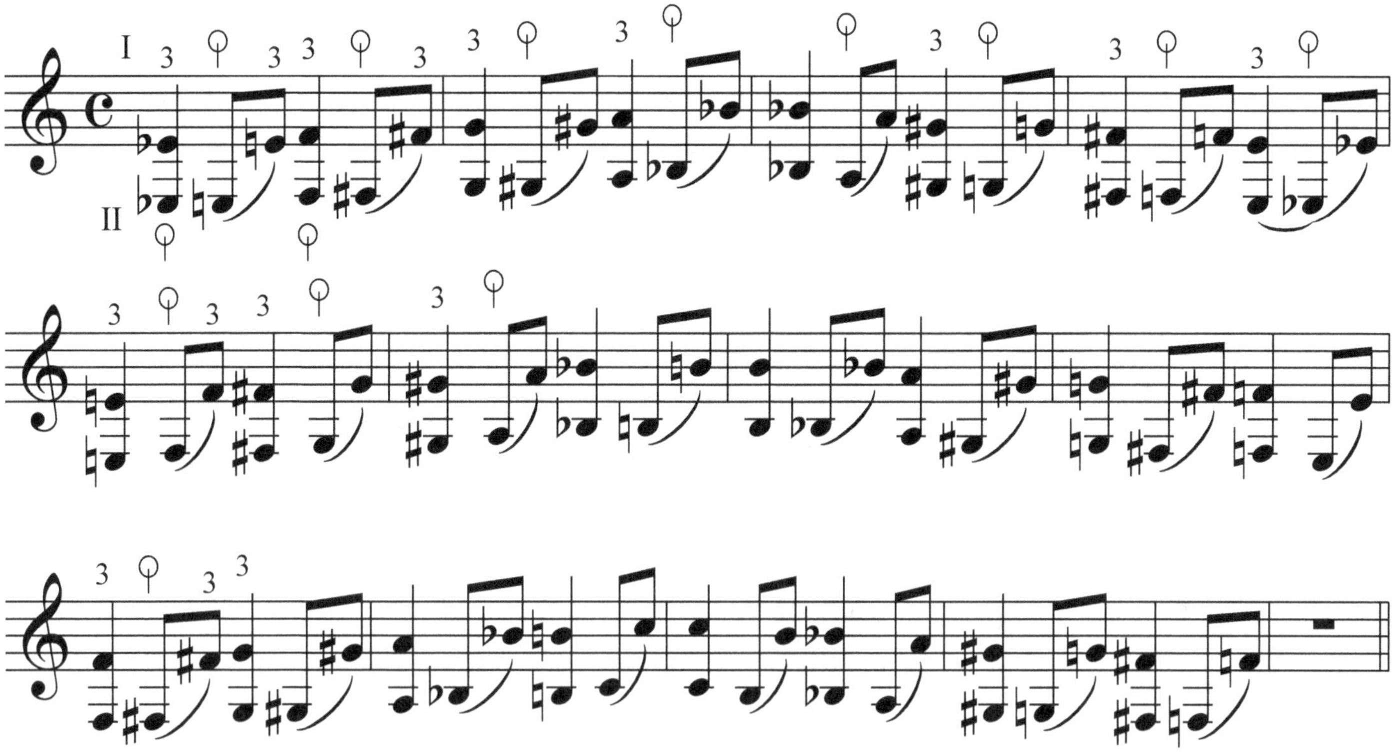

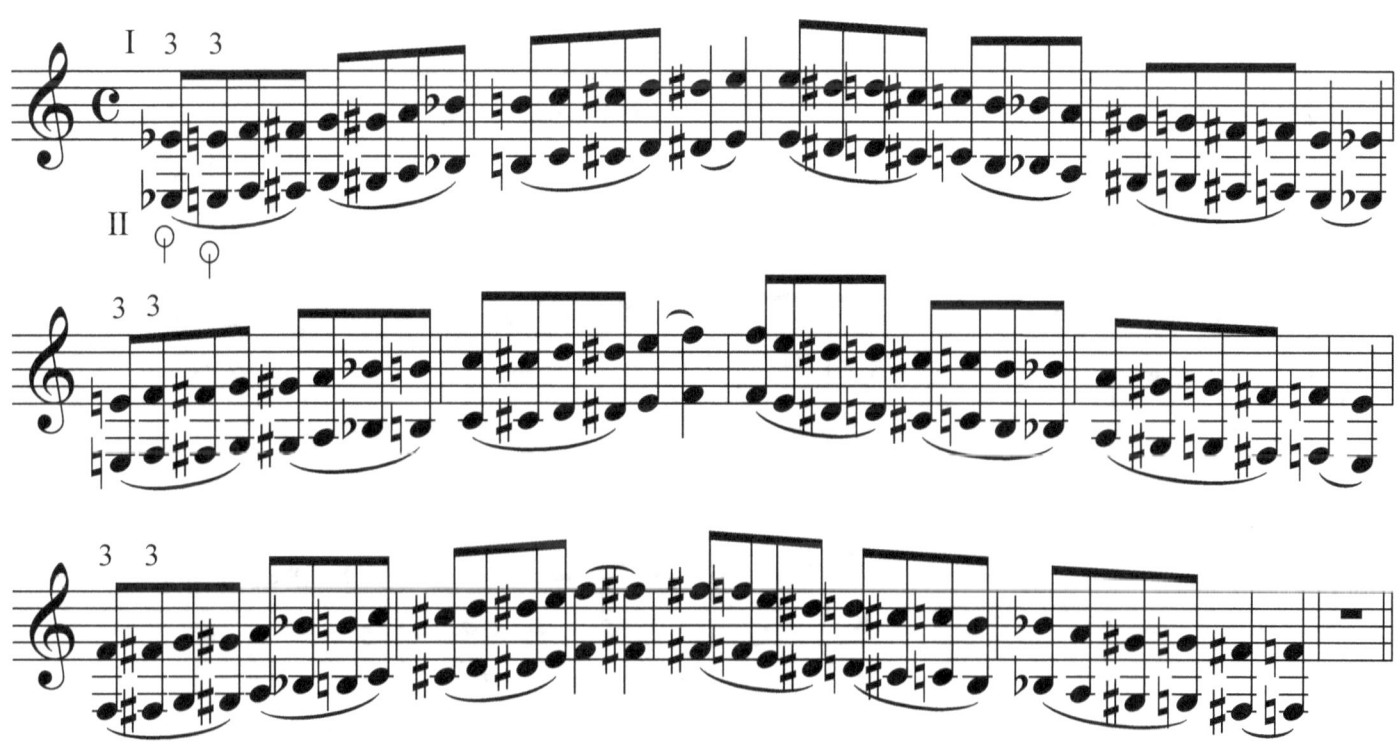

Continue playing the chromatic scales, starting a half step higher each time.

70

Continue playing the chromatic scales, starting a half step higher each time.

©2018 C. Harvey Publications All Rights Reserved.

71

Continue playing the chromatic scales, starting a half step higher each time.

72

Continue playing the chromatic scales, starting a half step higher each time.

Warm-Ups for the Advanced Cellist, Book One

The Lower Strings

73

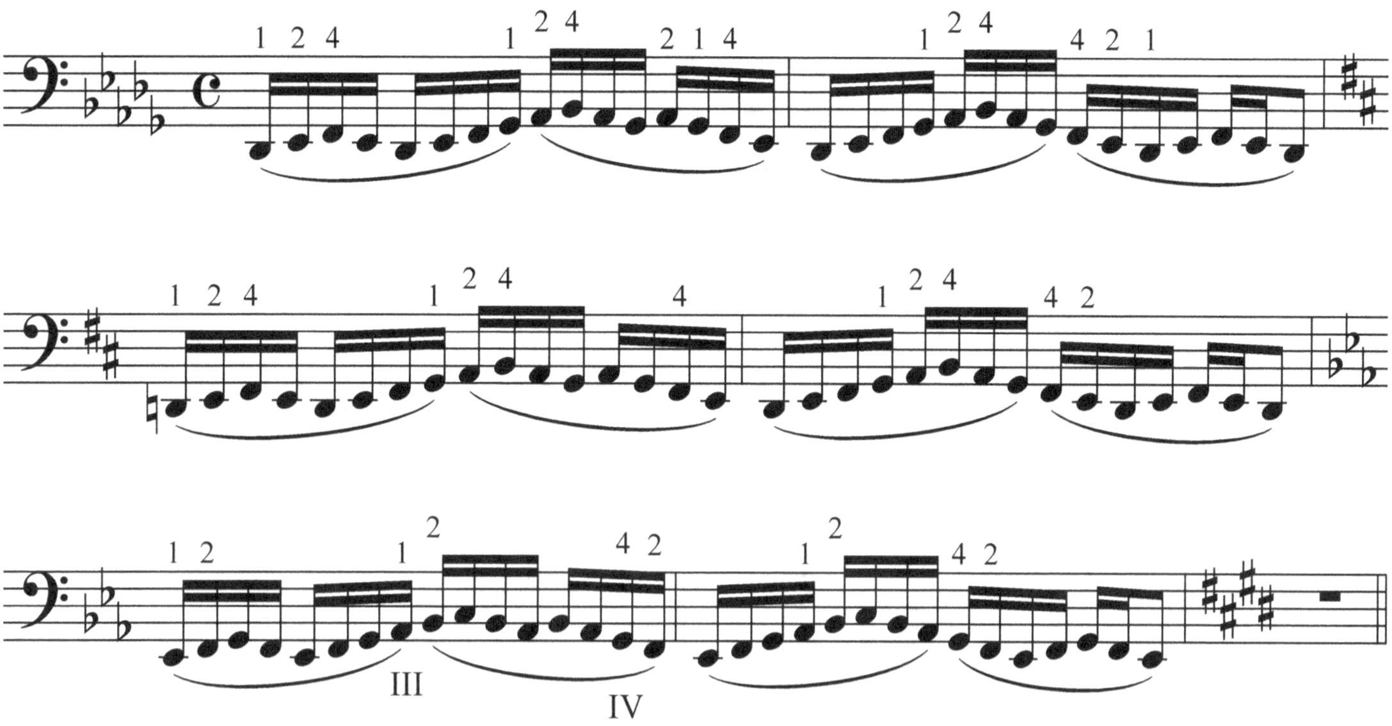

Continue playing the pattern, starting a half step higher and changing the key each time the pattern is played. Change strings where appropriate (usually after 4th or 5th position is reached on a string.)

74

Continue playing the pattern, starting a half step higher and changing the key each time the pattern is played. Change strings where appropriate (usually after 4th or 5th position is reached on a string.)

©2018 C. Harvey Publications All Rights Reserved.

75

Continue playing the pattern, starting a half step higher and changing the key each time the pattern is played. Change strings where appropriate (usually after 4th or 5th position is reached on a string.)

76

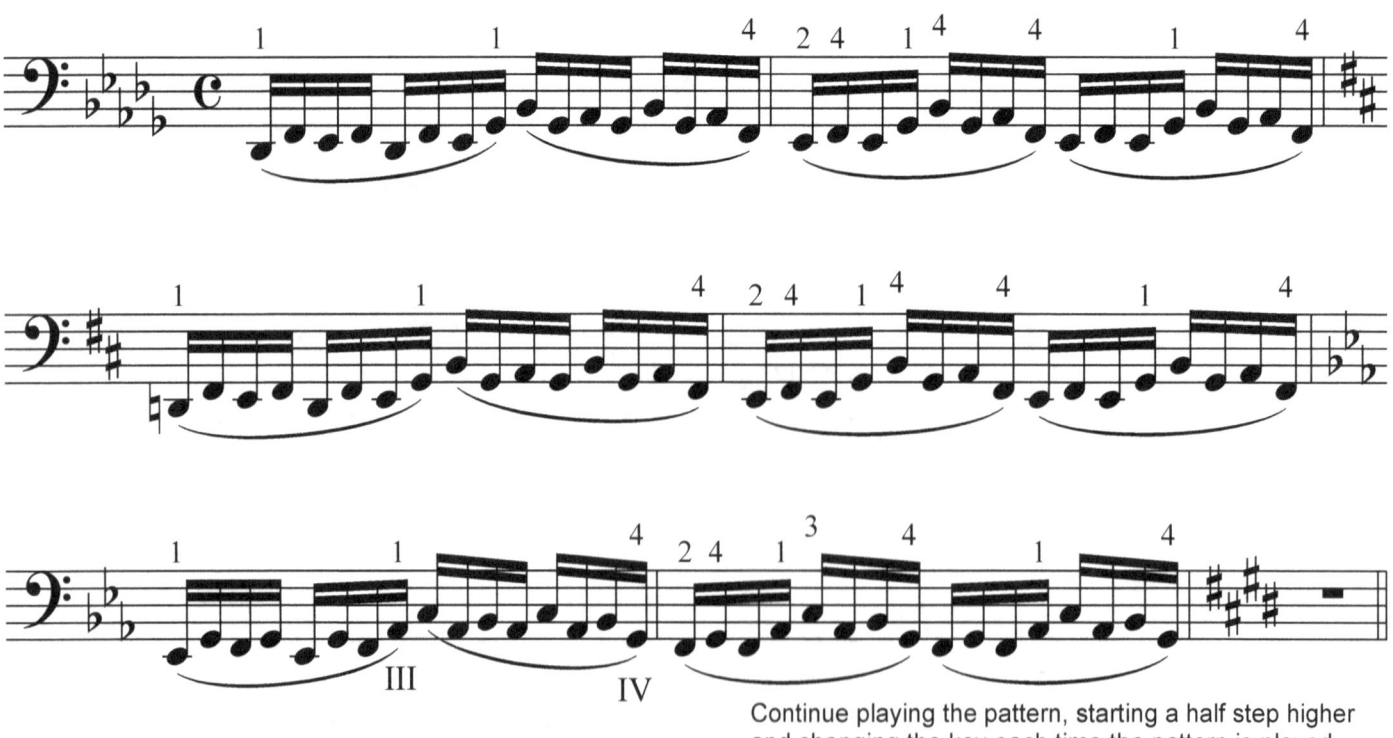

Continue playing the pattern, starting a half step higher and changing the key each time the pattern is played. Change strings where appropriate (usually after 4th or 5th position is reached on a string.)

Warm-Ups for the Advanced Cellist, Book One

77

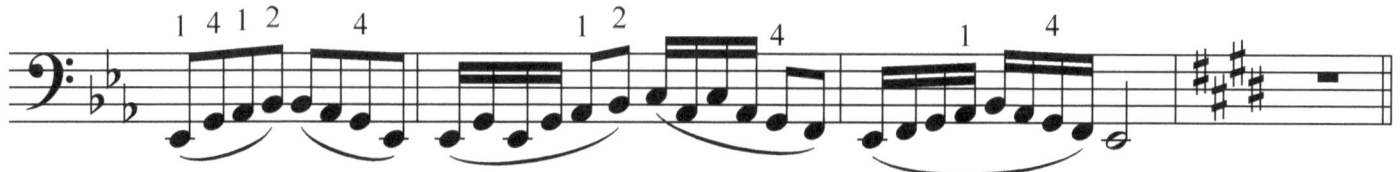

Continue playing the pattern, starting a half step higher and changing the key each time the pattern is played. Change strings where appropriate (usually after 4th or 5th position is reached on a string.)

78

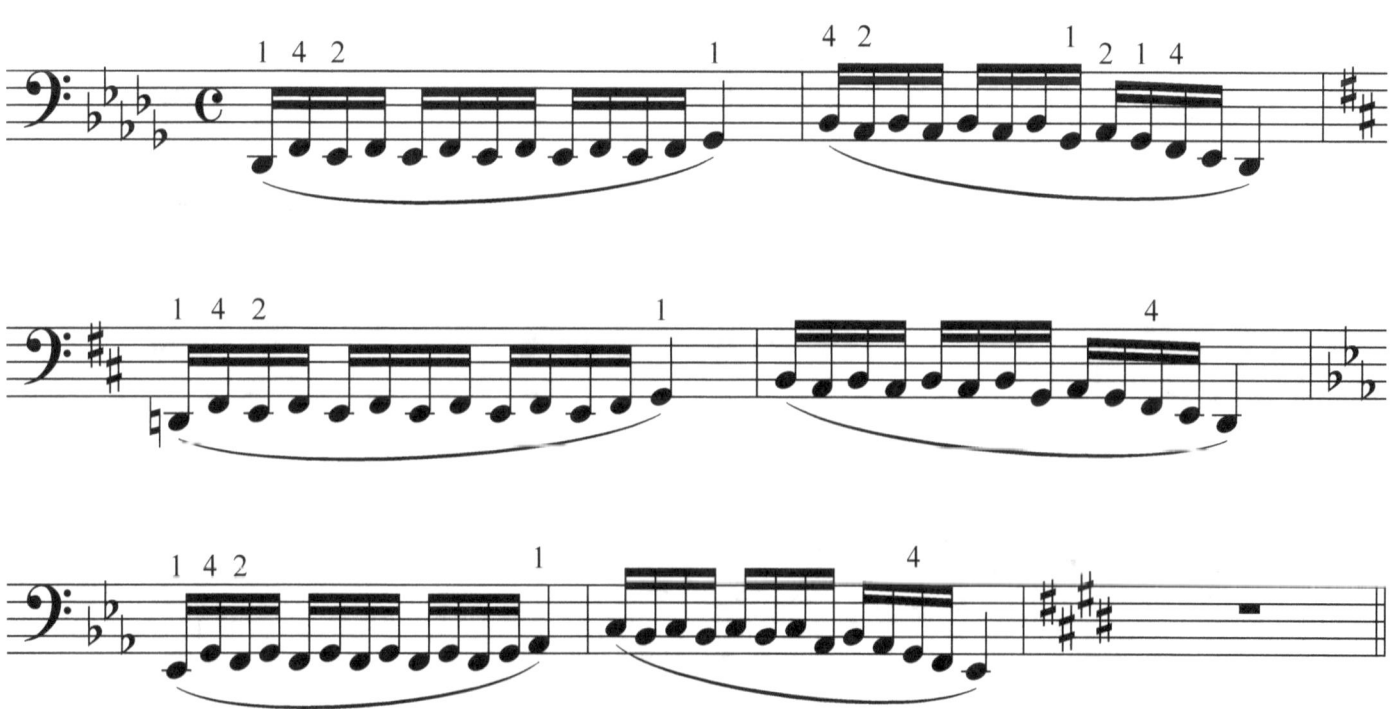

Continue playing the pattern, starting a half step higher and changing the key each time the pattern is played. Change strings where appropriate (usually after 4th or 5th position is reached on a string.)

©2018 C. Harvey Publications All Rights Reserved.

79

Continue playing the pattern, starting a half step higher and changing the key each time the pattern is played. Change strings where appropriate (usually after 4th or 5th position is reached on a string.)

80

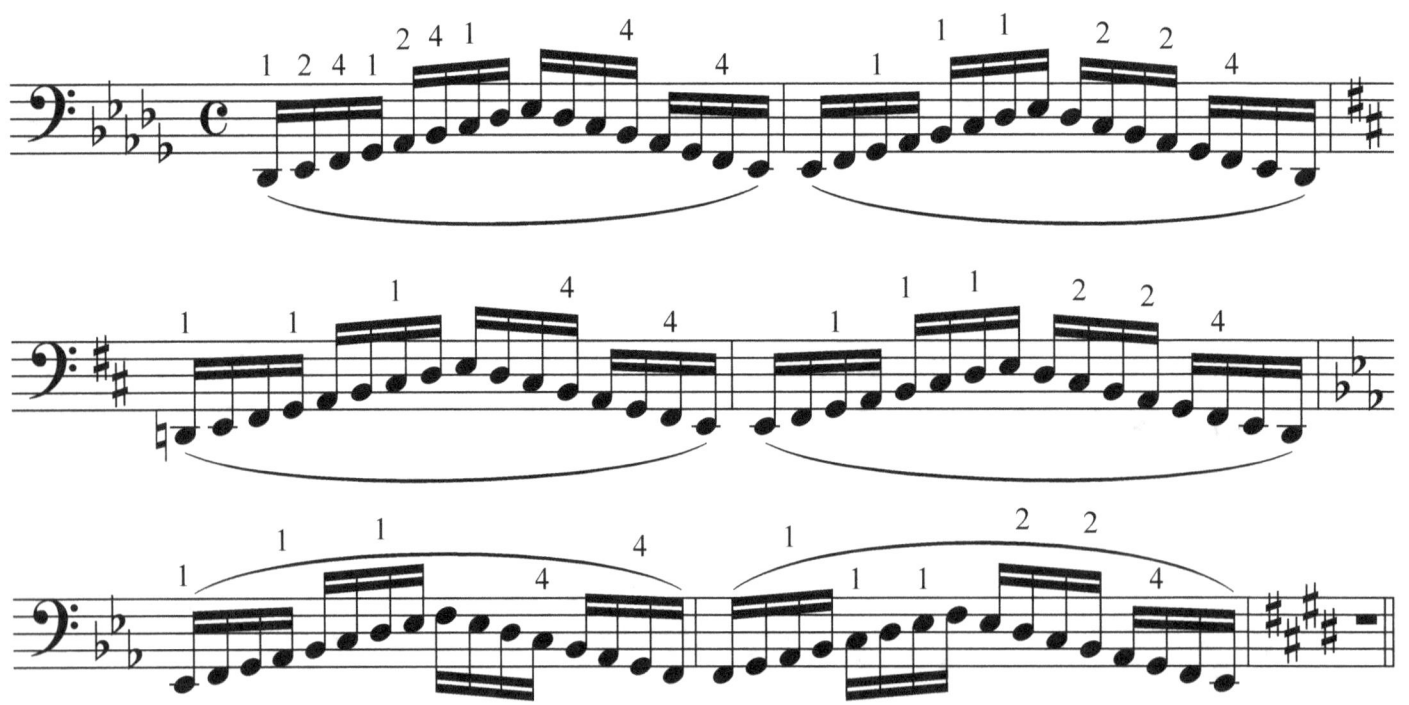

Continue playing the pattern, starting a half step higher and changing the key each time the pattern is played. Change strings where appropriate (usually after 4th or 5th position is reached on a string.)

©2018 C. Harvey Publications All Rights Reserved.

Warm-Ups for the Advanced Cellist, Book One

81

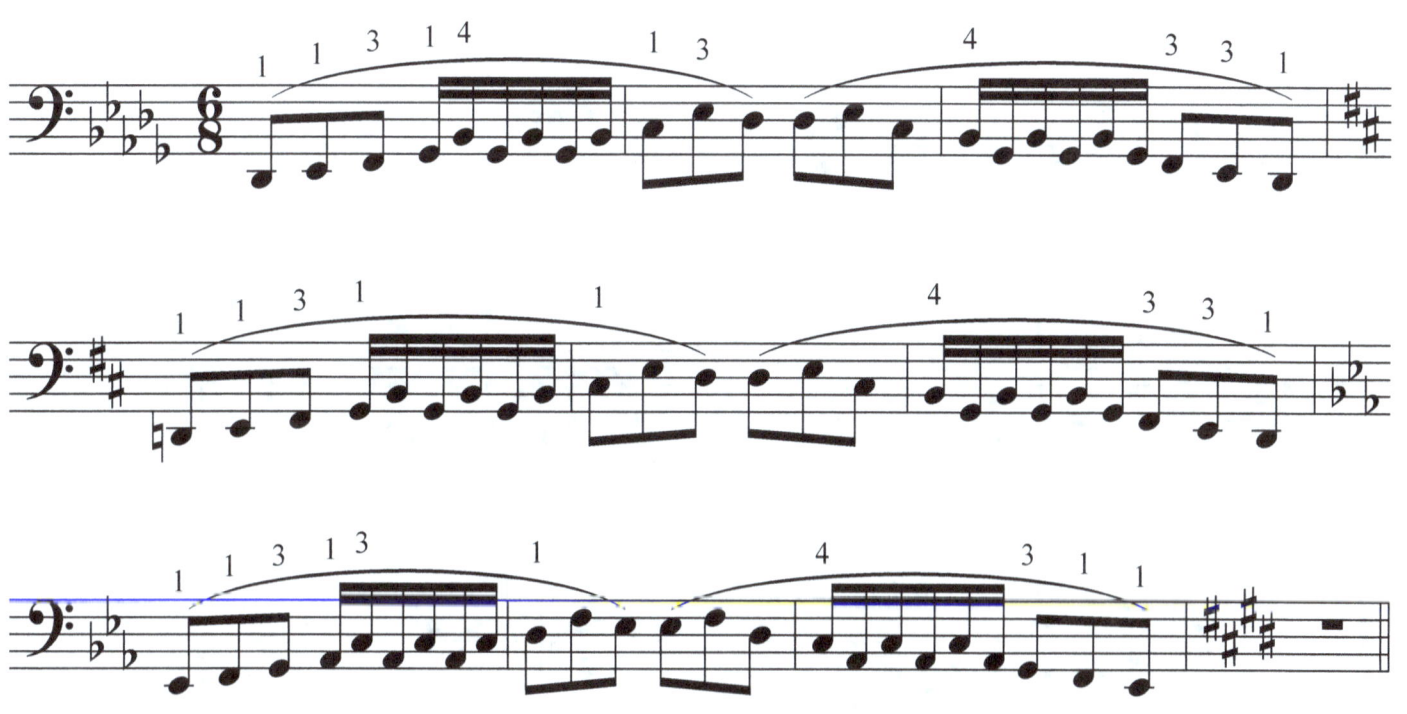

Continue playing the pattern, starting a half step higher and changing the key each time the pattern is played. Change strings where appropriate (usually after 4th or 5th position is reached on a string.)

82

Continue playing the pattern, starting a half step higher and changing the key each time the pattern is played. Change strings where appropriate (usually after 4th or 5th position is reached on a string.)

©2018 C. Harvey Publications All Rights Reserved.

83

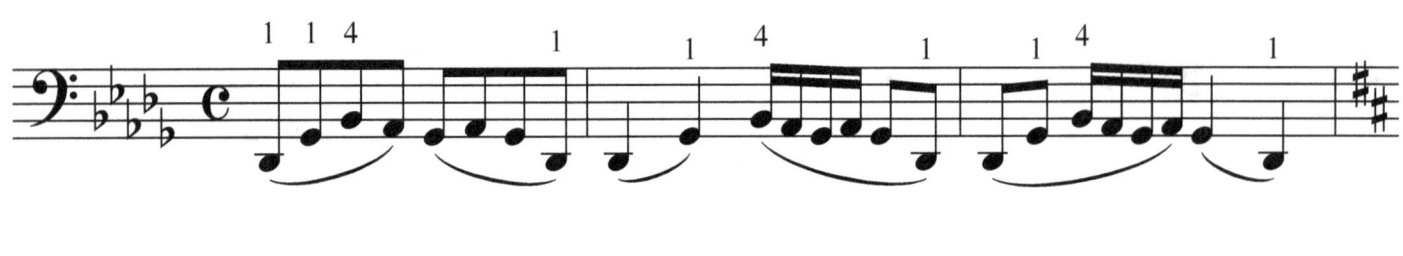

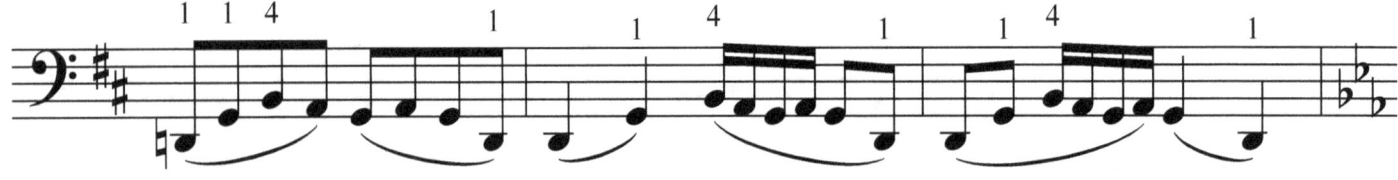

Continue playing the pattern, starting a half step higher and changing the key each time the pattern is played. Change strings where appropriate (usually after 4th or 5th position is reached on a string.)

84

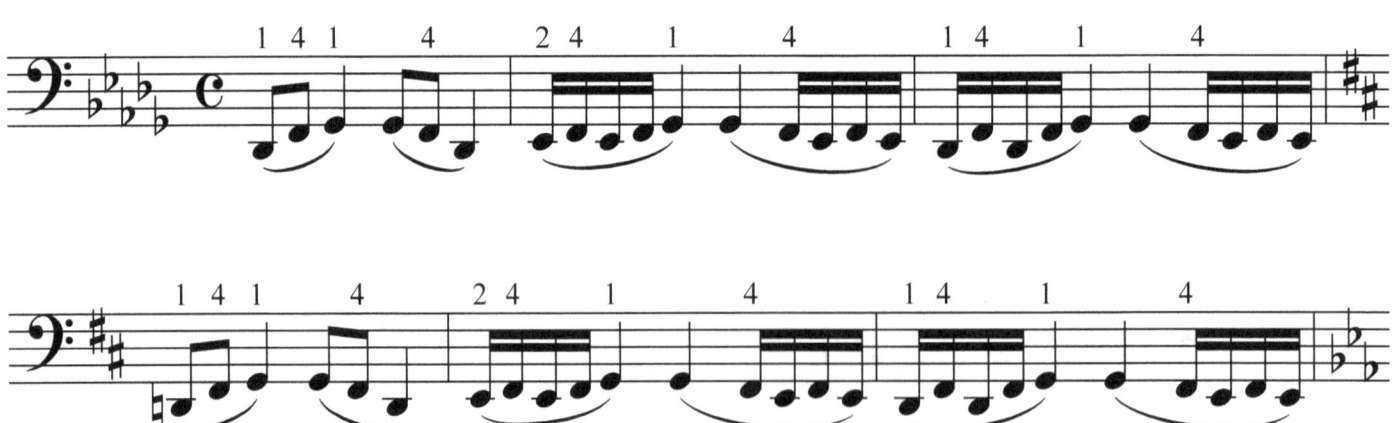

Continue playing the pattern, starting a half step higher and changing the key each time the pattern is played. Change strings where appropriate (usually after 4th or 5th position is reached on a string.)

Warm-Ups for the Advanced Cellist, Book One

85

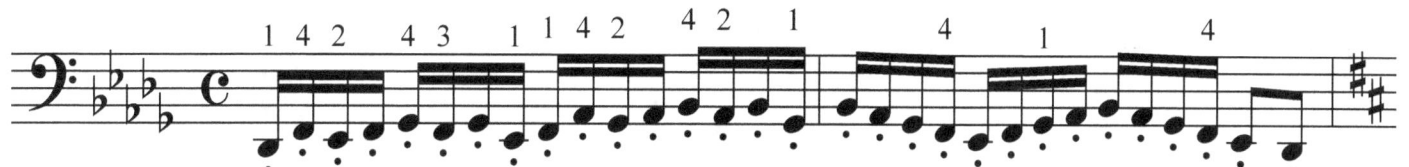
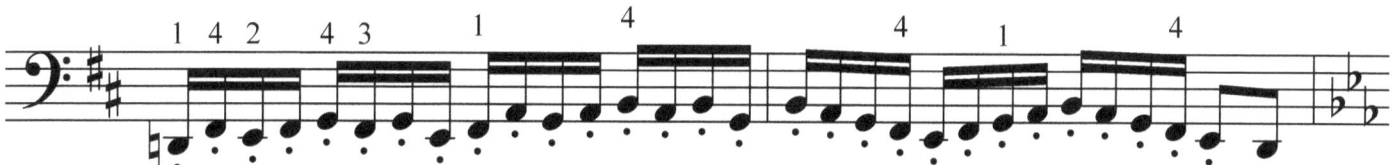

Continue playing the pattern, starting a half step higher and changing the key each time the pattern is played. Change strings where appropriate (usually after 4th or 5th position is reached on a string.)

86

Continue playing the pattern, starting a half step higher and changing the key each time the pattern is played. Change strings where appropriate (usually after 4th or 5th position is reached on a string.)

©2018 C. Harvey Publications All Rights Reserved.

87

Continue playing the pattern, starting a half step higher and changing the key each time the pattern is played. Change strings where appropriate (usually after 4th or 5th position is reached on a string.)

88

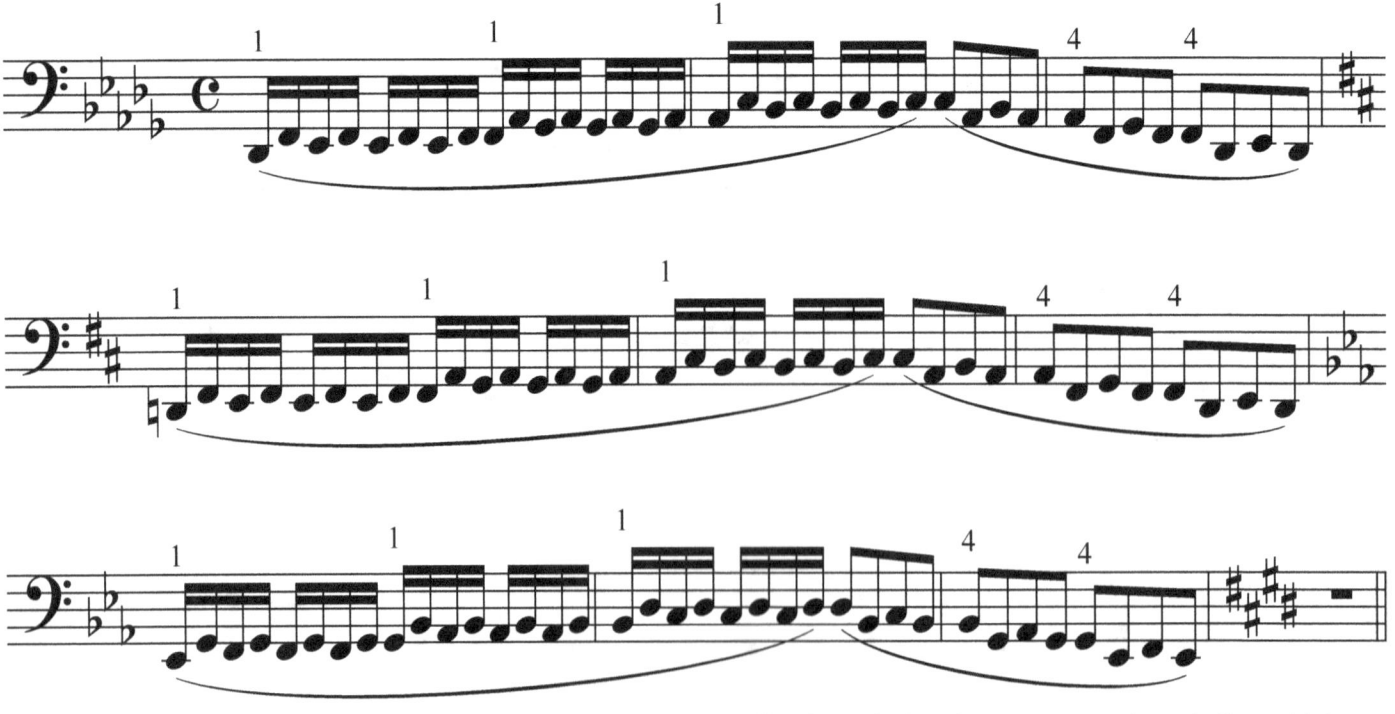

Continue playing the pattern, starting a half step higher and changing the key each time the pattern is played. Change strings where appropriate (usually after 4th or 5th position is reached on a string.)

©2018 C. Harvey Publications All Rights Reserved.

Warm-Ups for the Advanced Cellist, Book One

89

Continue playing the pattern, starting a half step higher and changing the key each time the pattern is played. Change strings where appropriate (usually after 4th or 5th position is reached on a string.)

90

Continue playing the pattern, starting a half step higher and changing the key each time the pattern is played. Change strings where appropriate (usually after 4th or 5th position is reached on a string.)

©2018 C. Harvey Publications All Rights Reserved.

91

Continue playing the pattern, starting a half step higher and changing the key each time the pattern is played. Change strings where appropriate (usually after 4th or 5th position is reached on a string.)

92

Continue playing the pattern, starting a half step higher and changing the key each time the pattern is played. Change strings where appropriate (usually after 4th or 5th position is reached on a string.)

©2018 C. Harvey Publications All Rights Reserved.

available from **www.charveypublications.com**: CHP211
Broken Thirds (One String) for the Cello, Book One

1

Cassia Harvey

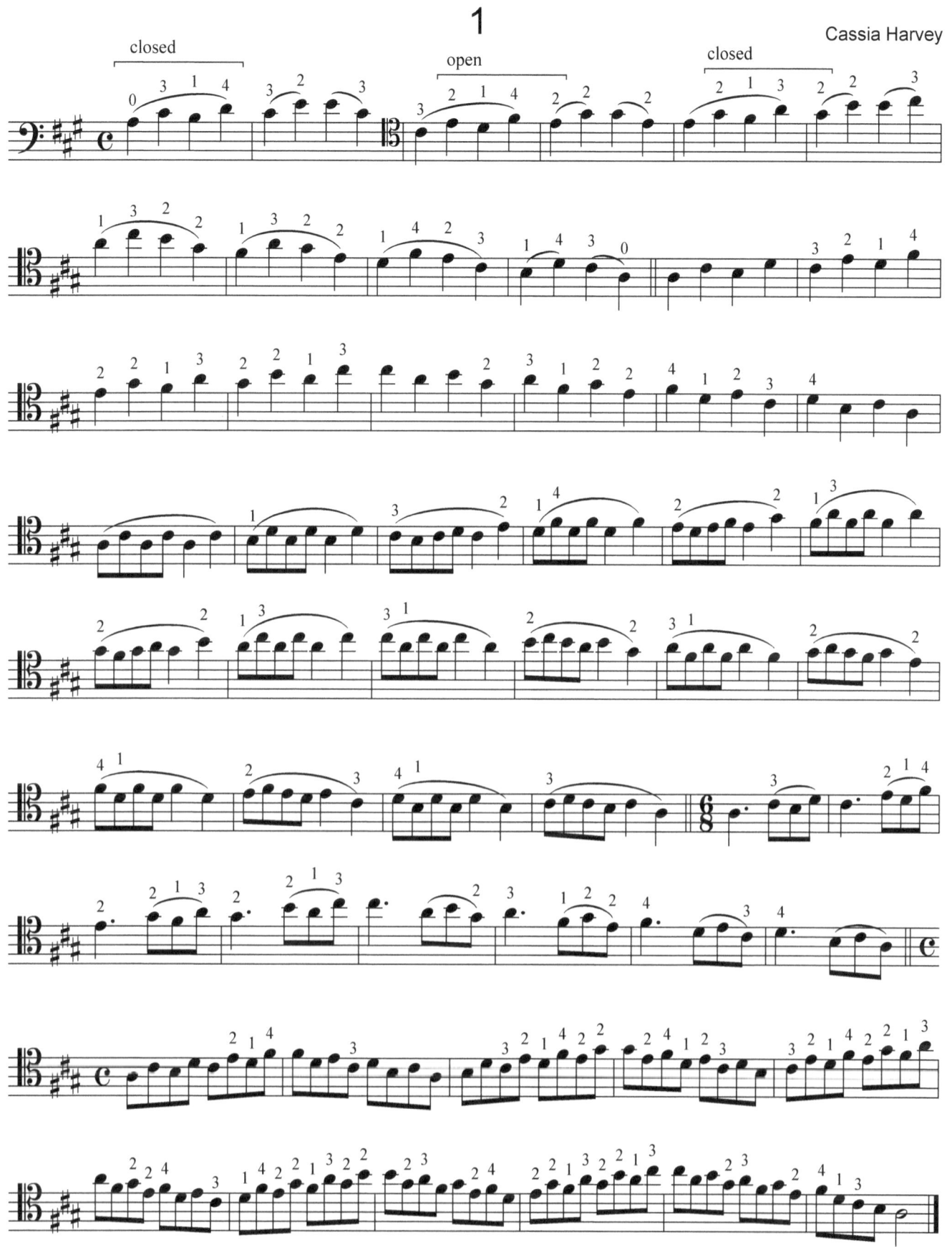

www.ingramcontent.com/pod-product-compliance
Lightning Source LLC
Chambersburg PA
CBHW080023130526
44591CB00036B/2615